ANGER

"A Misunderstood Emotion"

Reformers Unanimous International
PO Box 15732, Rockford, IL 61132
Visit our website at www.reformu.com.
Printed in Canada
Cover & Interior design by Benjamin A. Smith

ISBN 978-1-4276-4770-2

ANGER

"A Misunderstood Emotion"

FORWARD BY STEVEN B. CURINGTON

Dr. George T. Crabb, D.O.

TABLE OF CONTENTS

ANGER 6

nger

Of all the emotions, anger can be one of the most frustrating. It has a way of causing us to do and say things that we feel like we can never take back. In the wake of this destructive emotion you will find separation, depression, divorce, and emotional wounds that only God can heal. I can't think of a timelier topic to cover in this day than anger.

It's easy to identify rage in those who lose tempers in bad traffic, with unruly children, unresponsive coworkers, or unrealistic bosses. However, we must also recognize the more subtle manifestations of anger, such as anxiety, impatience, or being overly critical. These actions usually stem from the emotion of anger. Many fail to realize that the behavior causing such emotional bondage often originates from unrecognized and thus, unresolved pain or un-confessed sin from the past.

Are the negative emotions of angry people entirely avoidable? No, they are not. But they are coverable by the blood of the lamb and the word of a testimony. (Revelation 12:11)

Anger is a landmark book that strips away the myth and misconception about what causes aggressive angry outbursts and repressive implosions of angst. It will help you learn to distinguish between healthy and unhealthy anger so that you may choose—or help someone else to choose—God's plan for emotional well-being.

Anger examines the root causes of explosive patterns and breaks the destructive cycles of criticism, frustration, and irritation that hurt you and others around you. Using both the Bible and astounding medical insight, Dr. Crabb offers practical techniques to free us from anger and the angered. *Anger* is filled with real-life examples of the impact of anger and ways people have come to terms with their anger by applying these precepts.

Dr. George Crabb is a master at explaining complex ideas simply and biblically from a medical and spiritual perspective. Dr. Crabb tells us that, "Anger kills. Anger gets the best of people and brings out the worst in them." Dr. Crabb shows us in this book that the way to overcome anger is not to fight our emotions or to "let it all out" but to be transformed through the Word of God and Holy Spirit. *Anger* is a handbook not only for transforming anger, but also for living the victorious Christian Life.

Steven Curington

Founder and President
RU International, RU Homes
and Victorious Life
stevecurington.com

nger

INTRODUCTION

Anger is not only devastating our communities and churches, but it is dismantling the American workplace. According to the National Center for Victims of Crime website, more than two million people each year are victims of crime, with seventy-five percent of those cases being simple assaults. Workers, aged 35 to 49, are the most common targets, with 37 percent of them per year becoming victims of workplace violence. From 1994 to 1996, businesses ranked violence in the workplace as their number one concern *[National Center for Victims of Crime Website, "Statistics: Workplace Violence" 1998, p. 1; URL:http://www. ncvc.org/stats/wv.htm]*.

Why in these most recent decades has anger become so prevalent? We used to enjoy our home life, the workplace, the church home, the ministries, and just plain life! Why isn't life fun anymore? It seems that people are always under stress. It seems like people are always behind the eight ball. It seems like people are always being put on the spot with nowhere to escape or nowhere to obtain some type of rest. A recent Gallop Poll found that 49 percent of those surveyed generally experienced anger at work, with one out of six becoming so angry that he or she felt like hitting another person *[July 1999, Gallop Poll, Access Atlanta Website, URL:http://www.accessatlanta]*.

We used to escape the hostile work environment by retreating to the peace and sanity of our homes. However, this does not appear to be the answer anymore. Domestic violence is on the rise. And, it is not necessarily men becoming violent against women, but we are seeing an increased incidence of women becoming violent toward their husbands. It is believed that the true incidence of domestic violence is four million occurrences annually. Thirty percent of American women report that their husband or boyfriend has at one time or another physically abused them *[American Medical Association Website, "Facts About Family Violence", p. 1, URL:http//www.ama-assn.org]*. Violence in the home is not only limited to the adult partners but also includes the children. In 1995, for instance, nearly one million cases of child abuse were confirmed by Child Protective Services *[American Medical Association Website, "Facts About Family Violence", p. 2, URL:http//www.ama-assn. org]*. This statistic does not include the millions of incidents of angry outbursts, hateful words, and vicious looks, as well as the countless, unreported cases of neglect and abuse. If the character of a nation can be measured by its treatment of the young and elderly, then America would not be judged well. Reported cases of elder abuse rose 106 percent from 1986 to 1994, according to the National Center of Elder Abuse.

The American personality has distinctly changed over the past several decades. Instead of being a kind, compassionate nation, we are now a nation that is full of anger, frustration, impatience, and disrespect. The above, in general, defines the personality of America. We can see this in examples of road rage, rage at sporting events, and rage at a convenience store or grocery store. It appears the common theme of our civilization today is "rage." The thing that disturbs me the most is that too many of us feel that our anger or our outburst of rage is justified. This poses a very valid question: Do we have a right to be angry, or do we have the right to act out with the sense of rage? It seems to me that almost on a daily basis a new twist of anger either hits the printed communication or the television-cable media. Today, we have parents getting into fights at baseball games. We have people fighting each other to claim a spot in a grocery store parking lot. We have people fighting over the last copy of a magazine. It goes on and on and on! It almost seems as if our society has become one of these talk shows where people are blowing up at each other and getting into fist fights to "resolve the situation." As we look at this topic of anger, we must realize that there is nothing new about it; neither is the feeling of being justified in it.

Close to 3,000 years ago, we find a prophet of God by the name of Jonah sitting outside the city of Nineveh. Even though the city had repented of their sins, Jonah was sitting on the outskirts of the city hoping that God would still judge them for their ungodly ways. Jonah, I believe, was also preparing himself for a pity party if the Lord did not follow with the plan of judgment on the city. Jonah had found himself upset because the people of Nineveh had repented at his preaching, and Jonah knew that God, unlike himself, was a *"gracious God, and merciful, slow to anger, and of great kindness"* (Jonah 4:2). Jonah wanted the city utterly destroyed, but God seemed bent on sparing its residents if they would repent. They did repent! So, no judgment! Therefore, Jonah was angry.

God, then, asked Jonah a question. This is a question we need to ask ourselves. This question is found in Jonah 4:4, *"Doest thou well to be angry?"* Jonah tried to push aside the issue that God was putting His finger on. The Lord decided to give the prophet an object lesson. So, here is the rest of the story: Jonah 4:6-11 – *"And the LORD God prepared a gourd, and made it to come up over Jonah, that it might be a shadow over his head, to deliver him from his grief. So Jonah was exceeding glad of the gourd. But God prepared a worm when the morning rose the next day, and it smote the gourd that it withered. And it came to pass, when the sun did arise, that God prepared a vehement east wind; and the sun beat upon the head of Jonah, that he fainted, and wished in himself to die, and said, It is better for me to die than to live. And God said to Jonah, Doest thou well to be angry for the gourd? And he said, I do well to be angry, even unto death. Then said the LORD, Thou hast had pity on the gourd, for the which thou hast not laboured, neither madest it grow; which came up in a night, and perished in a night: And should not I spare Nineveh, that great city, wherein are more than sixscore thousand persons that cannot discern between their right hand and their left hand; and also much cattle?"*

As with most of us, Jonah's moods were based on the circumstances that surrounded him. When God "prepared a gourd" for shade, Jonah was happy. When God "prepared a worm" and "prepared a vehement east wind," Jonah was angry. When things were going his way, Jonah's anger was under control. But, it didn't take much to set it off again. This sounds very much like you and me. Jonah was understandably angry with the Ninevites because of their evil deeds that warranted God's judgment, but Jonah was unwilling to exercise grace and mercy toward them even when they repented. Jonah was aggravated with God because He chose to forgive the Ninevites. Finally, Jonah was furious with God because He took away his personal pleasure in regards to the gourd and turned up the thermostat in his life. Jonah was an angry man, and he was convinced that he had a right to be angry even if it killed him.

In this very revealing story of the life of Jonah, God demonstrated that Jonah cared more about his own comfort and the well being of a gourd than he did about the souls of people. Like Jonah, many of us today are stuck in our anger and subsequently are living a miserable Christian life.

In the New Testament the Apostle Paul warned that in the last days *"perilous times shall come"* (II Timothy 3:1). These perilous times denote times of arrogance and pride among the people. Paul goes on to tell Timothy of the life that is lived based on arrogance and pride with self-centered anger at its core. The following passage of Scripture really reads like today's newspaper headlines: II Timothy 3:2-4 – *"For men shall be lovers of their own selves, covetous, boasters, proud, blasphemers, disobedient to parents, unthankful, unholy, Without natural affection, trucebreakers, false accusers, incontinent, fierce, despisers of those that are good, Traitors, heady, highminded, lovers of pleasures more than lovers of God;"* USA Today puts it this way: "Leading social scientists say the nation is in the middle of an anger epidemic that, in its mildest form, is unsettling and at its worse turns deadly." I think if you were to ask the average person on the street what has changed about our society over the past several decades, a fair statement would be, "We have lost some of the glue holding our society together." In essence, they would be saying that we have lost our respect for one another. It seems as if the traditions of the past have been lost. No more is there a general respect for the elderly. There is not even a general respect for the dead anymore. In fact, simple respect for the living is no longer there either. Drivers who tailgate, cut off, and even attack other drivers are not seeing the others as neighbors to be loved as oneself. They have become opponents, obstacles, or even enemies.

Without a doubt, there are many circumstances that will either bring out our anger or will bring it out more vividly. The Bible is very clear that the root problem regarding anger lies within the human heart. Mark 7:14-15; 21-22 – *"And when he had called all the people unto him, he said unto them, Hearken unto me every one of you, and understand: There is nothing from without a man, that entering into him can defile him: but the things which come out of him, those are they that defile the man. For from within, out of the heart of men, proceed evil thoughts, adulteries, fornications, murders, Thefts, covetousness, wickedness, deceit, lasciviousness, an evil eye, blasphemy, pride, foolishness:"* Anger is truly a heart disease (the heart being the seat of our emotions and a part of our soul). In our ministry here at Reformers Unanimous International, almost, without exception, every individual that we deal with is having problems somewhere in their life with unresolved anger. As we take a step back and look at all of this unresolved anger, I believe an honest observation would be the following: The problem of bitterness and unforgiveness could very well be the most rampant, debilitating problem in the local church today. The anger epidemic which has crossed this world and has infected the American culture has very successfully infiltrated and infected the local church as well. We must realize as God's children that we have an adversary, and that adversary will seek to divide and conquer us at all cost. He will attempt to divide a human heart for *"a double-minded man is unstable in all of his ways"* according to James 1:8. Our adversary will attack our marriages, families, and churches.

He knows, according to Matthew 12:25, a *"house divided against itself shall not stand."* That is why when we look at the admonition to the Ephesian church by the Apostle Paul, we find it standing in sharp contrast to the spirit of resentment, hostility, and rage so evident in human cultures including the American culture of today. Paul says in Ephesians 4:25-27; 29-32, *"Wherefore putting away lying, speak every man truth with his neighbour: for we are members one of another. Be ye angry, and sin not: let not the sun go down upon your wrath: Neither give place to the devil. Let no corrupt communication proceed out of your mouth, but that which is good to the use of edifying, that it may minister grace unto the hearers. And grieve not the holy Spirit of God, whereby ye are sealed unto the day of redemption. Let all bitterness, and wrath, and anger, and clamour, and evil speaking, be put away from you, with all malice: And be ye kind one to another, tenderhearted, forgiving one another, even as God for Christ's sake hath forgiven you."*

Every night the sun will set on the unresolved anger of millions of people. This anger is toxic to the soul and rots the culture in which we live. The devil on one hand is delighted; and on the other hand, the Holy Spirit is grieved.

The following is a testimony from one of the men who was enrolled in our residential program here in Rockford, Illinois. This man was struggling with habitual, unresolved anger. In essence, he was addicted to anger. Ever since I was a little boy, I struggled with anger. During my childhood years, my father constantly criticized everything I did, and my friends picked on me relentlessly. As I now stand here by the grace of God, I realize that I have come a long way, but it still seems there are some strongholds in my mind over this matter of anger. I find that I really get upset if I feel mistreated or if I feel disrespected in any way. I have become much better in regards to not holding on to grudges as long as I used to. But, I am still having problems with the process of forgiveness. Many times,

I react so quickly to the situation around me that I don't even realize what I am doing. Normally these outbursts are full of anger and rage. I know that the problem is in my mind, but the negative thoughts seem to be so buried that I don't even know they are there. At this time in my recovery, I am simply praying that God would reveal the root causes of this bondage to me.

As I dedicate the time to writing this book, I do so in the attempt to help the individual who gave his testimony above find freedom from the bondage of anger. I desire to examine anger, to expose where it comes from, and then to compassionately show all of us how the Lord Jesus Christ can liberate you and me from anger's controlling influence. Anger in some way or form will always be a part of our lives this side of eternity. We cannot make anger completely disappear, nor should we even try for this to happen. There is a time and a place for anger. When we are walking in the *"liberty wherewith Christ hath made us free"* (Galatians 5:1), anger is our servant. However, when we are living a defeated life, a life of bondage, then anger becomes one of our masters. If we desire to be angry and sin not, then we need to be like our Lord Jesus Christ and be angry at sin.

Anger management is not the answer. All of the psycho babble out there is not the answer. Anger management trains the individual to keep the anger in a cage so it does not get out and cause harm to self and others. The goal is not to keep anger in a cage but to actually resolve the physical, soulical, and spiritual issues behind the anger. As we find and resolve the root of our anger, then and only then can we experience the fruit of the Spirit, which is *"love, joy, peace, longsuffering, gentleness, goodness, faith, meekness, temperance"* (Galatians 5:22-23). Those who are walking in the freedom of Jesus Christ don't cage up their anger and its associated destructive behavior, but they resolve the issue. Paul told the Romans in 12:21, *"Be not overcome of evil, but overcome evil with good."* This way of living sounds great! Would it not be wonderful to live a life free of ungodly anger? This way of life might sound too good to be true, but this life is real and attainable. I know you have struggled with anger all of your life and tried to overcome it. You never found the right equation that leads to lasting success. It always seems that the anger returned ending up mastering your life again. Or, you may be living with someone who is mastered by anger, whether it be your spouse or one of your children. Your body may even bear the scars of that anger or at least your soul does.

We at Reformers Unanimous want to teach you a whole new way of living that is full of freedom and absent of any anger that would be classified as sin. We desire to offer you hope, for there is hope in God. God can empower you through His indwelling Holy Spirit to control your anger and to properly respond to the anger of those around you. Don't feel hopeless. Look and mediate on the following verse that the Apostle Paul wrote to the Christians at Rome. Romans 15:13 – *"Now the God of hope fill you with all joy and peace in believing, that ye may abound in hope, through the power of the Holy Ghost."*

There is also the possibility that you like your anger. You use your anger to manipulate, intimidate, and dominate others. You like the control it gives you over other people, including your spouse, child or children, and parents. As a child, you threw tantrums. But now, as an adult, you have become more sophisticated with your tantrums. You raise your voice and lower your gauge and even possibly make threats. You thrive on the fear your anger imposes on others. As a drug addict gets high off their drug, you get high off your drug called anger. Anger may be getting you what you think you need, but ungodly anger will never give you what you really need because *"the wrath of man worketh not the righteousness of God"* (James 1:20).

You will come to find out that the most angry people are the most insecure people in the world. They use their anger to control and manipulate others to make them feel more secure. This type of life filled with anger is a sickness of the soul and body that only the truth (Jesus Christ) can overcome. Jesus Christ can make you free according to John 8:32 – *"And ye shall know the truth, and the truth shall make you free."* He can make you free from ungodly anger. Jesus not only wants to give you life eternal, but He wants to give you a life *"more abundant"* as noted in John 10:10. Jesus Christ will make you free of ungodly anger and give you a peace that you have longed for. This peace that Jesus Christ gives is different than what the world can give you. John 14:27 – *"Peace I leave with you, my peace I give unto you: not as the world giveth, give I unto you. Let not your heart be troubled, neither let it be afraid."* The peace that Jesus gives goes beyond human understanding. Philippians 4:6-7 – *"Be careful for nothing; but in every thing by prayer and supplication with thanksgiving let your requests be made known unto God. And the peace of God, which passeth all understanding, shall keep your hearts and minds through Christ Jesus."* This peace that God speaks of is a powerful peace, and this peace can reign in your life – YES! Your life! God can and will fill us with peace where once only anger existed. This life is a life of true freedom and a life worth pursuing.

As we continue looking at this issue of anger in depth, we will see how it affects our body, soul, and spirit. You see, like most things in life, they affect the whole person: body (physical), soul (mind, will, and emotions) and spirit (spiritual part of our lives). We will demonstrate that there is a war going on for your soul, and you can control your emotions through the truth, which is the Lord Jesus Christ.

My friend, there is no greater joy than to allow the Holy Spirit to take your anger from you and make you the child of God He desires you to be. Jesus will make you free and set you apart to serve Him. Let's take this journey together and see the Lord Jesus Christ uplifted in our lives.

ANGER 18

nger
CHAPTER ONE:
HOW IT WORKS

A young lady here in Rockford, Illinois, whom we will call Susie, has come to our Women's School of Discipleship because of trouble in her family. She states that for the majority of her life, anger was always a part of her existence. Her father, you see, had an anger problem; and because of this anger problem, the whole family was disrupted, the family ending in divorce. Most of the lives in the family were destroyed. Susie would tell of days when her father would come home from work and bring all the frustration and anger with him. It got so bad that many times her mother would find herself in deep depression and lay in bed for days at a time just to get away from her husband and not deal with the situation. Susie would run to her room to avoid her father. He would run after her, chasing her and screaming at her. At times, he would hit her and pull her hair. There were several events when Susie and her siblings would run to the police station because their father was chasing them and threatening to do bodily harm.

Susie not only grew up with this outwardly manifested anger, but she also dealt with the depressive effect it had on her mother. In fact, Susie had to deal with the trauma of finding her mother after she had attempted suicide. Fortunately, Susie found her mother in time, and she was able to be revived. Susie, growing up in this difficult situation, to say the least, believes that her father's anger is one of the bigger reasons why she became rebellious in regards to her walk with God and other authority figures. She continued to see her father (her authority figure) acting up in an ungodly manner, demonstrating ungodly anger with absolutely no compassion whatsoever. This is the devastation that anger can have on oneself as well as those around them.

What was going on inside of the body of Susie's father? How was he responding to all of the frustrating circumstances he found at work as well as the ultimate anger that he demonstrated in his own life? The thought and feelings running through his brain were sending a signal deep into his brain to the area called the hypothalamus.

For this next section, we will call Susie's father by the name of Robert. We must ask ourselves the question: What was going on in Robert's body as he dealt with all this frustration and anger? Robert's anger was running wild through his cerebral cortex sending signals even deeper into his brain called the hypothalamus. The hypothalamus, being activated by these signals of anger, stimulated the sympathetic nervous system, which, in turn, restricts the arteries which carries blood to every vital organ of his body, including his heart, lungs, kidneys, and skin. As all of this is going on, the brain is sending a hormonal signal to the adrenal glands to release large quantities of adrenalin (epinephrine and norepinephrine) and Corte sol (our body's own natural steroid) into his blood system. As Robert confronted his family with his anger, his neck muscles tightened, his blood pressure rose, and his heart rate increased. The muscles in his stomach and intestines constricted down which caused him to experience abdominal pain and cramping. Robert's skin felt cool and clammy because blood was being directed away from it so more blood could go to the muscles to facilitate the "fight or flight" response that God has engrained in all of us.

Robert's body was preparing to go into action; but in many instances, no action was ever taken. The adrenalin released into his body stimulated his fat cells to empty their contents into his blood stream for a potential energy source. But, instead,

Robert, for the most part, just sat there fuming inside with his body converting the fat into cholesterol. Most of time, he had no one to fight and nowhere to take flight. Robert, for most of his days with anger, felt trapped. As Robert continues to have bouts of anger with no external release, the cholesterol formed from the unused fat in his blood stream will potentially accumulate forming deadly plaque in his arteries that will one day lead to a stroke, heart attack, or even facilitate kidney failure as well as causing premature death.

In all practical purposes, anger kills. Anger gets the best of people and brings out the worst in them. This is even more noticed when jealousy enters the mix. Proverbs 27:4 – "Wrath is cruel, and anger is outrageous; but who is able to stand before envy?" Regardless of the weapon used, the threat of violence has our nation on edge. There is an undercurrent of hostility in our nation, community, churches, and families that make us focus on everything else but Jesus Christ. Numerous people are at their breaking point and who knows when the slightest mishap will set them off on a deadly rampage. With all this said, please remember that anger kills.

Many studies have shown how anger affects our lives in an adverse way. In the medical profession, stress is considered to be the major cause of life-threatening illnesses. In fact, those with a hostile personality are more prone to coronary artery disease. A cynical distrust of others, the frequent experience of angry feelings and the overt expression of cynicism in aggressive behavior had a higher incidence of developing life-threatening diseases than their less-hostile counterparts. People prone to anger are also more likely to engage in risky behavior like eating more, alcohol use, and tobacco abuse; all of which are known to damage our health and diminish longevity. In my medical opinion, people do die from psychosomatic illnesses. This indicates that more is going on in our bodies than just a response to life on the physical plane.

We must reckon with the non-physical aspect of our being, which includes our soul and spirit. To understand how the body, soul, and spirit interact, we must go back and see how God created us in His own image. When God formed Adam from the dust of the ground (physical), He then breathed into him the breath of life (the spirit), and then man became a living soul (soulical). Every human being is a trichotomy (body, soul, and spirit). We are both material (body) and immaterial (soul and spirit). Our body is the material part, and it relates to the world around it through the five senses God gave it. The soul (the mind, will, and emotions) and spirit are the immaterial part. As we are created in the image of God, we have the ability to think, feel, and choose (soul) and commune with God (spirit). God so delicately has woven the material part of us to the immaterial part, making us three in one (or a trichotomy). God has made the outer person and the inner person to work together in beautiful harmony. The greatest of illustrations is the brain (physical) and the mind (soul). There is a fundamental difference between the brain and the mind. The brain is an organic piece of tissue that is part of our material body. This "piece of equipment" can be likened to the hard drive or the hardware of a computer. The mind is part of the immaterial aspect of our being (the soul – the mind, will, and emotions). It can be likened to the software of the computer. Using this picture we can see that the brain (hardware) and the mind (software) are no good without each other. We also come to see that the brain (hardware) cannot function any way other than how it has been programmed. This programming comes by the mind (software). The brain (hardware) is the central nervous system with its 12 cranial nerves along with the spinal cord. Branching off the central nervous system is the peripheral nervous system that has two distinct divisions.

The first division is what is called the somatic nervous system. The somatic nervous system helps regulate all of our muscular and skeletal movements. It is that which we have control over. The somatic nervous system would be used in this way. If we decided to kick a ball with out right foot, we would mentally choose to kick the ball with our right foot, and our body would respond by doing so. We can choose to walk, run, clap, smile, or frown. The somatic nervous system takes orders from our will, which is a part of the soul. We don't do anything without first thinking it. The thought-action response may be so rapid that we are hardly aware of the sequence, but it is always there. However, involuntary movements (tremors) do occur when the system has an imbalance, as is the case with Parkinson's disease (an imbalance of the neurotransmitters dopamine and acetylcholine in the substania nigra of the brain).

The second division of the peripheral nervous system is the autonomic nervous system which we do not have volitional control over. The autonomic nervous system works together with our emotions (part of the soul). The autonomic nervous system deals with the regulation of our internal body, which includes our heart rate, digestion, bowl, and bladder control, etc. We do not have control over the autonomic nervous system just as we don't have control over our emotions (like anger). We cannot will ourselves to like people we have emotional hatred for. We can choose to do the loving thing for them even though we don't like them. We cannot simply tell ourselves to not be angry because we can't directly manage our emotions that way. When we admit we are angry, we can have control through the Holy Spirit on how we are going to express it. We can keep our behavior Christ-like because we have control over our behavior. Also, we have control of what we think and believe and that is what controls what we do and how we feel. We do a similar thing when we talk with angry people.

Telling an angry person they don't have to feel or act that way produces only guilt or defensiveness. But, we can encourage them to manage their emotions better. If you go about just telling them not to be angry, you will have as much success as telling them to control their autonomic nervous system (which, as you know, cannot be done). We must realize that what is causing the autonomic nervous system to respond this way is not the brain (the physical body), and it is not the brain that is causing us to feel angry. It is the mind (soul), and the way it has been programmed. The circumstances surrounding us or the people around us do not make us angry. Our perception of those circumstances and those people and how we interpret them will determine whether we will be angry or not. All of this is a function of our mind, a part of our soul, and how it has been programmed.

Let's look at a stressful situation and how our bodies respond to it. When we experience pressure in life, our body automatically tries to adapt. Our adrenal glands secrete epinephrine and norepinephrine as well as Corte sol into our blood stream helping us to meet the challenge ahead. But, if the pressure persists too long, stress becomes distress and our system breaks down and we become sick. Suppose two doctors had a setback; their company or private corporation got sued. The one doctor is a nonbeliever in Jesus Christ and sees this situation as devastating to their referral business. He believes the news of the pending lawsuit will decrease referrals, thus, bankrupt the business. His dreams are dashed. The doctor acts angrily toward anyone who tries to console him. The other doctor is a believer in the Lord Jesus Christ and truly believes that success lies in an individual following God's will for his life. He believes God is in total control and will meet his every need. The lawsuit has little impact on him, for he believes God is in this to further His will in his life. Of course, the doctor is disappointed, but he does not get angry. This doctor sees an opportunity to trust God and then sit back and watch God work. On the one hand, you have the first doctor totally stressed out and angry, and on the other hand, you have the other doctor experiencing very little stress and absolutely no anger. Can belief in Jesus Christ make that type of difference in how we look at things and how we act toward our circumstances? The answer is a resounding YES! The difference between the two doctors is not their physical makeup but their soulical makeup (or their belief system). Proverbs 23:7 – "For as he thinketh in his heart, so is he: Eat and drink, saith he to thee; but his heart is not with thee."

How we behave depends upon what we believe. Like all of our emotions, anger is a product of our thought-life. Suppose you are at the post office one day and an individual bumps into you and knocks you down with that individual landing on top of you. You may initially think the person is careless and in a rush and that thought leads you to the emotion of anger. Your body (physical) will respond in the "fight or flight" response. Your adrenal glands will begin to secrete epinephrine and norepinephrine and Corte sol into your blood stream to prepare you for a possible confrontation. If your senses tell you it was some young kids just playing around, you are more likely to pick yourself up and go about your business. However, your anger is a natural response to how your soul (mind) interprets the data that is being picked up by your five senses. How you feel depends on the data you receive and how your soul (mind) interprets that data. This brings up a thought that we must examine. If what we believe does not conform to the truth, then what we feel does not conform to reality. Suppose a husband comes home angry at his wife for spending a lot of money that day on clothes when they are on a very tight budget. The man had heard from one of his friends that their wives went out shopping together and that his wife had spent a lot of money that day. As it turned out, the wife did no such thing. The husband was angry because he believed it to be true. The man is now no longer angry at his wife, but he is probably a little bit angry at his friend.

You see, it is not the actual circumstance that triggers our physiological response. The adrenal glands do not decide on their own to secrete epinephrine, norepinephrine and Corte sol. The truth is the circumstances surrounding us are picked up by our five senses and sent as neurochemical signals to the brain (body). The soul (mind, will, and emotions) then takes the information, makes an interpretation, which leads to choices being made. The choices made in our souls (mind, will, and emotions) are what determines the neurochemical signal that is sent from the brain (body) to the peripheral nervous system to the muscular skeletal system of the body. The brain, which is a part of our body, cannot function any other way than in the way it has been programmed by the mind, which is a part of the soul. This is why we are transformed by the renewing of our minds. Romans 12:2 – "And be not conformed to this world: but be ye transformed by the renewing of your mind, that ye may prove what is that good, and acceptable, and perfect, will of God."

How our soul (mind, will, and emotions) has been programmed is revealed by our belief system, which reflects our values and attitudes about life. What we believe does affect how we respond to the circumstances of life. If our identity and security is firmly established in the Lord Jesus Christ, then the things of this life have less of an impact on us. As we are conformed to this image of God, we will become a little less angry and a little more like Jesus Christ.

———————————

nger

CHAPTER TWO:
GOD'S WILL VS. GODLY EXPECTATIONS

It was one of those days that I had at the office, busy from beginning to end, and it seemed like nothing came easy. All things demanded a challenge by me and my staff. In light of this, I dreamed of going home and having a nice, quiet dinner with my family. Sitting down at the dinner table, my expectations were, to say the least, very high. However, my two year old son did not have the same mindset that I did that night. He did not like what mom fixed for dinner, so he began to fuss and squirm as did I at his actions. My reaction to him just fueled his behavior; and by the time I knew it, we were in an uproar at the kitchen table. After we finally finished dinner, I stomped off into the family room to watch the evening news. A little while later my wife came to me and whispered in my ear, "You should not get mad at your son like that!" Her tone of voice was insistent, and it got my attention quickly. The Holy Spirit of God also got my attention. I was convicted of my ungodly anger that I displayed in front of those I loved and cherished the most. I told my wife she was right, and I apologized to both her and my son. I also sought God's forgiveness, which He so graciously granted me. God wasn't done with me. He prompted me to ask myself a question: Why did I get so angry at my son? All I wanted was a nice, quiet dinner around the kitchen table with my family. But, my son did not cooperate, and I got angry when the events of the evening did not go my way.

God immediately reminded me that the fruit of the Spirit is temperance, which is God controlling me and not me controlling my spouse or children. By angrily trying to control others so I could fulfill my own purpose or satisfy my own expectation for comfort, I was not acting in agape love. God still wasn't done teaching me out of the situation that just occurred. God made me contemplate on why I got so angry at my son for not eating the food in front of him. When I angrily yelled at him, he just cried louder, making the situation even worse. God, then, convicted me of the lie that I was holding onto that I could persuade anybody of my point of view and get them to do what I thought was right. That lie is not only arrogant but futile as well, especially with an irrational, screaming, two-year-old boy. According to Jesus, the joy of living does not come from getting my way but by doing the will of the Heavenly Father. John 15:10-11 – *"If ye keep my commandments, ye shall abide in my love; even as I have kept my Father's commandments, and abide in his love. These things have I spoken unto you, that my joy might remain in you, and that your joy might be full."*

All of us can look back and find times when we responded poorly to life's situations and gave way to angry behavior. As we look at these episodes and examine them, we come to find out that our personalities and temperaments have something to do with how we responded. Some people are more naturally laid back while others are just task driven. Most individuals find themselves somewhere between the two extremes. However, the expression of anger is not just related to our personalities and our temperaments, but it is also strongly related to what we believe right now as we react to others and the circumstances surrounding us.

Webster's 1828 Dictionary gives this definition of *anger*: *"A violent passion of the mind exceeded by real or supposed injury; usually accompanied with a propensity to take vengeance or to obtain satisfaction from the offending party. Anger may be inflamed until it rises to rage and a temporary delirium."* The two Greek New Testament words often translated as "anger" and "wrath" are *orge* and *thumos*, respectively. Strong's Concordance gives an explanation of the difference between the two words. In the New Testament the Greek word *thumos* is used eighteen times and it is used seven times in the book of Revelation in reference to God's wrath. Every other time, *thumos* is used in the New Testament to indicate a sinful human behavior.

Paul gives us a strong warning from God in Ephesians 4:31 – *"Let all bitterness, and wrath, and anger, and clamour, and evil speaking, be put away from you, with all malice:"* Now, we know that anger is part of our natural emotional makeup (part of our soul), but this verse makes it crystal clear that Christians have no business holding onto or meditating upon anger in their hearts. If this was not the case, why would Paul be so firm about the need to get rid of all of it (orge and thumos). The question that must be posed and properly answered is: Why do we get angry anyway?

The following is a list of why people get angry:

Injustices in Life
Such righteous indignation is justified and is similar to the wrath of God and is spoken of more times in the Bible than the anger of mankind. Godly anger becomes a powerful motivating tool to correct social injustices.

Do Not Get Your Way
King Ahab wanted Naboth's vineyard. When Naboth refused to trade or sell, Ahab went home *"heavy and displeased…and he laid him down upon his bed, and turned away his face and would eat no bread"* (I Kings 21:4). We often see this in children. Their wills get crossed and explode; but unfortunately, the problem is not limited to children as Ahab demonstrated. No matter what our age or status, when we don't get what we want, our natural response is anger.

Things Seem Out of Your Control
The more Saul lost control over David, the shorter his temper became. Praise for David shocked Saul's ego like an earthquake. The more Saul sought to eliminate David the more miserable

he failed, and Saul became a very frustrated, angry man. Most of us will not readily identify with Saul. He is the bad person in the story. We identify with David. But, under our masks we are more like Saul than we want to admit. When people do things that threaten our securities or slight our egos, our efforts to counteract them only result in more of the same. Frustration over situations and people we cannot change eats at us like a cancer.

Need to Control
This is only an extension of the former reason. Saul, like many of us, learned that anger makes people back off and often give in. It even makes some people cater to you. A loud voice, a fist on the table, as well as a lethal glare keeps others hopping. Anger controls! Rather than face the difficulty of confrontation with an angry person, most people bend.

Response to Hurt or Mistreatment
When David and his men were rebuffed by Nabel, David put on his sword and set out to annihilate the whole tribe. David's reaction was typical. Sharp, sudden pain always triggers curses and unleashes blind rage. It matters little if the pain is physical or emotional. Vengeance anger grows little by little over years of mistreatment; and once a wound is opened, the angry person may become extremely touchy. Slight mistreatment, even words or actions not intended to hurt, can trigger angry reactions.

Wounded Pride
The Bible records that King Asa faced a hoard of invading Ethiopians that outnumbered the Israelite army two to one. Asa humbly sought the Lord. God not only gave him a tremendous victory but also brought a great revival among the Israelites. Many from the Northern tribes went over to Asa *"when they saw that the LORD his God was with him"* (II Chronicles 15:9). Shortly after this, however, and perhaps in retaliation for political fallout, Baasha, King of the Northern tribes, came against Asa. This time Asa sent a "league payment" to the Syrian King, Ben-hadad, to get him to break off his agreement

with Baasha and form a union with Asa instead. It worked! However, Hanani, a prophet of God, rebuked Asa for relying on a heathen king instead of relying on the Lord. Asa's response: II Chronicles 6:10 – *"Then Asa was wroth with the seer, and put him in a prison house; for he was in a rage with him because of this thing. And Asa oppressed some of the people the same time."* How could Asa switch so rapidly from urging people to follow the Lord to lashing out at the ungodly? Someone touched his ego; that's why! Asa's pride, founded on his spiritual progress, made it all the more subtle. Out of wounded pride a minister may make an angry reply to a just criticism, or a father may lash out at children who see through his mistakes. Wounded pride hurts!

Spill Over From Unresolved Guilt
David was guilty of immorality and covered up murder. When he was told a story about a rich man who took advantage of a poor man, he exploded. Covered sin makes us touchy. A man who secretly looks at pornography or attends peep shows will almost invariably be harsh with his children. A person who lives with a guilty conscience often wills a criticizing tongue. Such a person is continually engaged in the subconscious task of trying to transfer his guilt to someone else.

Physical Conditions (Acute, Chronic Pain; Weariness; Sickness)
The above physical situations leave us emotionally depleted unless able to control our anger. Many times individuals who are suffering will try to medicate themselves. The use and misuse of alcohol, prescription drugs, and street drugs to try and numb the pains of life is rampant. I see this all too often in my medical practice day in and day out. All too often, their use opens a Pandora's Box of volatile emotions and violent anger.

To Set Things Right
We all have a sense of justice. When David heard about the rich man taking his poor neighbor's only sheep to feed unexpected guests, he was angry. Rightly so! There is righteousness in this kind of anger. When a situation is wrong, anger is a motivation

to set things right. Moses saw the lewdness of the calf-worshipping Israelites and was furious. Jesus saw the irreverence of the money changers in the Temple and took decisive action. When we see two big boys beating up on a little boy, we have the same emotional response. We call it righteous indignation, and it is!

We all have heard the term "monkey see, monkey do." This applies a lot to our children. They are awesome observers but poor interpreters of what they observe. They have no problem mimicking the behavior they hear or see. Our children, therefore, are vulnerable to picking up and demonstrating the anger of their parents or caregivers. Our anger as parents sows seeds of rejection in our children at young ages, and many children will not wait until adulthood to express that anger. Many children are showered with seeds of rejection until they are overwhelmed by an environment that is hostile and cruel.

In recent years, we have seen these bitter seeds bare staggering, deadly fruit as young people have exploded in violence. We must understand that for a child his or her "world" is primarily the home in which they live. Children that grow up in a home where the sense of steady-flow rejection comes day in and day are given a message loud and clear – You are worthless! You are stupid! You are a loser! You are unwanted! They truly are unloved, and they know it! A sense of rejection will yield a deep-seated anger in the rejected child's heart, which is the seat of his or her emotion and the part of his or her soul.

The problem with all of this is that all of the above can be hidden behind the walls of a seemingly normal family. I find this can happen in mainly *four different ways*: (1) *Perfectionism:* This is parents who impose unrealistic goals on their children. Children in this environment learn quickly that they are not good enough. No wonder that end up viewing themselves as worthless. (2) *Overindulgence:* If a child is given everything growing up, they can quickly become angry at a world that will not bow at their command when they grow up. (3) *Overprotection:* This can communicate to the child that they are weak and not prepared to face the world and its challenges. (4) *Performance-based acceptance:* This is acceptance with strings attached. It is conditional love and not agape love. I will love you "IF YOU...." Unfortunately, this is the driving force behind many people, and some are successful. No matter how this performance-based acccptance is looked at, it is not acceptance at all – IT IS REJECTION!

Like all other reasons for rejection, it can cause a child to feel worthless, unwanted, and extremely angry at everyone around them. These children generally grow up and are highly driven, trying to beat the system, and in the process, often become angry controllers of all that are around them. Many others will rebel against the system in deep anger and bitterness. They make it look like they don't want your love, acceptance and approval. But, down deep they desperately need it. The character we all have is most affected by the presence or absence of unconditional, agape love in our homes.

The Bible has numerous illustrations where individuals provoked others to anger:

1. Esau was angry at Jacob because he deceived him out of his father's blessing (Genesis 27:41-46).

2. Jacob was angry at Laban for treating him unfairly (Genesis 31:36).

3. Potiphar was angry at Joseph because he believed his friend had betrayed a deep trust they shared (Genesis 39:19).

4. Miriam and Aaron were angry with Moses out of envy (Numbers 12).

In each of the cases above, these people's anger was based on something or someone that they had no right or ability to control.

Realistically, we all have certain expectations of ourselves and others with the hope that the circumstances surrounding us will allow us to carry out our plans in life. But, many times, circumstances do not cooperate, and, sometimes, others do not properly participate. At other times, we, ourselves, do not properly comply with our plans in life. If we believe that our identity and sense of worth depends upon the cooperation of others and upon favorable circumstances, then we will likely try to control them. When we find out that we cannot control others and that we cannot control the circumstances surrounding us, we will have the tendency to get angry at others. If the outcome feels uncertain, we get anxious. If the desired goal seems impossible to achieve, we get depressed.

We need to make a distinction between God's will for our lives and Godly expectations that we have. These are two distinctly different things. No one or no thing can disrupt God's will from being done in our lives except if we fail to follow His Divine plan for our lives. Regardless of what His will is, it is doable because *"with God all things are possible"* (Matthew 19:26), and *"I can do all things through Christ which strengtheneth me"* (Philippians 4:13). If God wants it done in our lives, then it can be done! Whatever God requires us to do, we can do by His grace.

So, let's make the distinction between the two. God's will is basically anything that reflects God's purpose for our lives, independent upon people or circumstances beyond our ability to control. God's will for our lives is for us to become more like His Son, Jesus Christ. This process is called sanctification and is demonstrated in Paul's writing to the Christians at Thessalonia in I Thessalonians 4:3 – *"For this is the will of God, even your sanctification, that ye should abstain from fornication:"* No circumstance or person can stop us from being the person God created us to be. We are the only ones who can disrupt God's will from being done in our lives. What an awesome responsibility! However, if we believe that God's will in our lives depends upon other people or the circumstances that surround us, then we will be filled with anxiety, depression, and anger.

We know that not all circumstances will be favorable toward us and not every person we run across will be promoting godliness in our lives. We also know that we do not have the right nor the ability to control the circumstances or the people surrounding us.

Now, compare this with a Godly expectation. A Godly expectation does depend on favorable circumstances or the cooperation of others whom we have no right or ability to control. The problems come when we equate a Godly expectation with God's will for our lives. ILLUSTRATION: You are in a rush to get home to take your wife out to dinner. You have a reservation at six o'clock. However, you must first stop and get gas for the car. Of all days, there is a backup at the pump, and the line you pull into has a little old man taking his time filling his gas tank and cleaning his windows. You become frustrated at the delay you are experiencing, and you find yourself getting angry. That little old man is blocking your expectation of a wonderful, relaxing evening with your wife. But, that elderly man does not determine who you are. How you respond to that elderly man will reveal your flesh patterns and your belief systems. Patience is a fruit of the Spirit; and if you were walking in the Spirit, patience would be evident. In the above illustration, you have a Godly expectation of taking your wife out to dinner and being on time; however, you have elevated it to God's will for your life, and that is driving you into a state of rage and anger.

Suppose your Godly expectation is to have a loving, happy, Godly home? Who can block that goal? Everyone in the family! This is a legitimate, Godly expectation, but you cannot control everyone in your family every moment of every day. If you try to make this happen by controlling the other family members, then there will be a lot of angry people in your household. However, it is God's will for you to become the parent and the spouse God designed you to be, and no one can block that but you!

So, we see that if someone or something comes along and

prevents us from achieving our plans, we get mad. We see that person or circumstance in an adversarial way that it or they are making life more difficult for us, and we react in anger. If the person or circumstance appears threatening to us, the intensity and duration of our anger will be greater. You can tell how important a goal is to you by how much you are angered and how long you stay angry. We have a choice, thank God! We can have an outburst of anger according to our old flesh patterns, or we can respond by the empowering of the Holy Spirit of God by faith. Instead of becoming anxious, stressed out, or depressed over a goal that seems impossible, we can have love, joy, and peace. Instead of anger ruling our hearts, we can have the patience of God. We can have joyful endurance in the midst of frustrating circumstances. We can actually grow through the trials of life and become more like Jesus Christ. If you find that the difficulties in your life are making you angry, then consider what Paul wrote to the Christians at Rome. Romans 5:3-5 – *"And not only so, but we glory in tribulations also: knowing that tribulation worketh patience; And patience, experience; and experience, hope: And hope maketh not ashamed; because the love of God is shed abroad in our hearts by the Holy Ghost which is given unto us."*

The pressures of life help to reveal wrong goals, but they make possible God's goals for our lives, which is for His children walking in the Spirit. We are able to grow to be more like Him through every crisis in life. What if your Godly expectation isn't met? We will feel disappointed. We must remember that life will not always go our way, and the people around us will not always respond in a Godly fashion. This does not determine who we are. God has already determined who we are. We are His children bought with the shed blood of Jesus Christ. We are in the process of being changed into the image of His dear Son. Nobody or nothing can keep that from happening; only we can keep that from happening.

---

nge
CHAPTER THREE:
BE YE ANGRY & SIN NOT

Numerous times in the Bible we are taught that difficulties and trials in our lives are designed to produce a Christ-like quality in us. They are there to make us more like Jesus Christ. Through trials, we can become better men and women for God; however, there is another side to this coin. Trials make people bitter! We come to see that God uses trials as one of His main tools to accomplish His will in our lives. When we do not accept God's will as our will, then we end up viewing difficult times as a test of God's love for us rather than a test of our own character.

With anger we cry out to God or verbally lash out at others rather than being able to give thanks as Paul commanded us to do in I Thessalonians 5:18 – *"In every thing give thanks: for this is the will of God in Christ Jesus concerning you."* If we allow our anger to turn into bitterness, we can significantly hinder the work of God in our lives. At this juncture of the book you might be saying, "So what do you expect me to do when I find out I owe the IRS $10,000? Am I supposed to thank God or something?" As a matter of fact, that is exactly what the Bible is saying to do. Otherwise, it is to invite anger, anxiety, and depression to take control rather than the Spirit of God. When we are thankful in situations as mentioned above, it demonstrates faith, and it is a powerful diffuser of anger. It shows that you have accepted God's will for your life and that is to become more like His Son everyday. Instead of giving into your anger, use it as a diagnostic tool to indicate the probable presence of a selfish or worldly goal rather than a Godly one. By doing this, you can learn from your mistakes rather than just repeating them. You see, wrong goals may be good desires that have become too important to us. It is something we feel we can't or don't want to live without. When this occurs, the goal becomes our god – an idol. An idol is anything we look to before or in the place of God to meet our needs or satisfy our souls. If we believe the lie that we need the approval of others in order for our needs to be met, then we will seek out to gain their approval. The more difficult it is to obtain their approval, the harder we will go after it. My friends, we already know that trying to manipulate and control others will not meet our needs or satisfy our souls or even make us happy. What will happen is that as we encounter unfavorable circumstances in people who do not meet our expectations, anger will set in. We must realize that as believers in Jesus Christ, we are loved, accepted, and approved by God the Father already. If we fail to realize this or somehow forget this wonderful aspect of our salvation, then we will try to meet those needs through other people.

The Apostle Paul wrote in Galatians 1:10 – *"For do I now persuade men, or God? or do I seek to please men? for if I yet pleased men, I should not be the servant of Christ."* Those that seek to please people are a slave of other people and not of Christ. This is keenly seen when we are rejected by a loved one such as a parent, child, or spouse. These instances are the most emotionally volatile. The closer the relationship the more painful the wounding and the greater potential for anger. I believe it is normal to hurt and to experience anger when someone we love doesn't love us in return. Not all anger is the result of wrong goals being blocked. Sometimes, we experience anger because we have been genuinely hurt. Everybody has a built-in sense of justice as to what they perceive is right or wrong. Look what happens when one person's idea of justice doesn't agree with another person's idea of justice. When they both have strong ideas of justice, the situation will only lead to a heated, if not angry, exchange.

Anger also comes in response to a perceived violation of one's rights or by someone else not living up to their responsibility. When our rights are violated, we call that abuse. When someone fails to properly care and provide for those they are responsible for, we call it neglect. We get angry when we perceive others or even ourselves being abused or neglected. If our perception is proper and our judgment is correct, then our anger is righteous.

A young mom and her two-year-old son were in my office one day. I was taking care of the mother's medical needs when the son got into my canister of cotton balls and threw them everywhere. The mother got up from the examining table and grabbed the boy by his arm and dragged him over to one of the chairs. She started yelling at him using cruel, demeaning names. I immediately felt outraged over the damage being done to that child. That is righteous anger, and it ought to prompt you and me to take action. The above is a true case of abuse. Therefore, anger is legitimate as long as the Spirit of God leads any subsequent action you take.

We should get angry when we encounter abuse or neglect. Righteous anger consists in getting angry at the things that anger God and then seeking a proper remedy to correct the wrong. Jesus was a perfect example of this when He cleansed the temple. Matthew 21:13 – *"And said unto them, It is written, My house shall be called the house of prayer; but ye have made it a den of thieves."* Jesus was righteously angry at the defamation of God's glory in His temple, and He did something about it. If you want to get angry and sin not, you must get angry like Jesus did. GET ANGRY AT SIN! Jesus forcefully put a stop to the sinful behavior, but He did not hurt the sinner.

On one Saturday, Jesus entered the synagogue and saw a man with a withered hand. Jesus' enemies watched Him closely to see if He would heal on the Sabbath day. When Jesus asked them, *"Is it lawful to do good on the sabbath days, or to do evil? to save life, or to kill?"* (Mark 3:4), they had nothing to say. The Lord *"looked round about on them with anger, being grieved for the hardness of their hearts,"* (Mark 3:5) and proceeded to heal the man with the withered hand. Jesus was angry at the Pharisees who valued their religious traditions so much more than a human life. The Pharisees showed complete neglect of the disabled man's need for mercy, love, compassion, and healing. So, Jesus became angry in accordance with the righteous anger of God. That anger moved Him to do what was right.

Unfortunately, all anger is not as righteous as the Lord Jesus was. Too many times, we wrongly judge others and react in anger when they fail to live up to our expectations. Righteous anger that does not result in righteous action may lead to cynicism and bitterness. Righteous anger should always lead us to do something righteous, something constructive, and something good, like forgive, pray, fast, alleviate suffering, etc. When we simply stew in our indignation, we develop a bitter spirit. Psalm 37:8 says, *"Cease from anger, and forsake wrath: fret not thyself in any wise to do evil."*

Let's look at the difference between assertive anger and hostile or aggressive anger. Assertive anger flows out of righteous anger. This is what we experience when people invade our personal space, threaten our rights, or violate the emotional or physical boundaries of ourselves or others. Hostile or aggressive anger seeks to do harm; assertive anger is designed to firmly say, "This far and no farther!" This is not selfish or an unloving thing to do at all. It is rather the opposite. When we set limits on what we allow others to do by exercising assertive anger, the door remains open for love. If we fail to take action; however, we find ourselves growing increasingly irritable, frustrated, and resentful. There are frequent opportunities to express assertive anger toward those who knowingly or unknowingly take advantage of others. In doing so, we need to speak the truth in love (Ephesians 4:15 – *"But speaking the truth in love, may grow up into him in all things, which is the head, even Christ:"*) and have the other person's best interest at heart. The goal is not to get even but to correct the wrong so all are built up. Many in the Christian community have been taught that any and all anger is sin. This is not the truth. Ephesians 4:26 says, *"Be ye angry, and sin not: let not the sun go down upon your wrath:"*

We may perceive a person or circumstance to be wrong, which may generate an initial reaction of anger in our soul. However, we do not have to act on that emotion, and we do not have to act sinfully. We do not have control over our autonomic nervous system (the initial reaction of anger). We do, however, have control over what we think (soul) and do (soul telling the body what to do).

Cain chose to act in anger when his sacrifice was rejected by God while his brother's sacrifice of an animal was accepted. This is the first incident of anger in the Bible. It is found in Genesis 4:5-7 – *"But unto Cain and to his offering he had not respect. And Cain was very wroth, and his countenance fell. And the LORD said unto Cain, Why art thou wroth? and why is thy countenance fallen? If thou doest well, shalt thou not be accepted? and if thou doest not well, sin lieth at the door. And unto thee shall be his desire, and thou shalt rule over him."* Cain disobeyed when he brought his offering *"of the fruit of the ground"* (Genesis 4:3). God rejected this offering. Cain, having felt this rejection, probably felt the following in his body: Cain's adrenal glands would have been stimulated by his feeling of rejection. His adrenal glands would be pumping excess epinephrine and norepinephrine into his blood system, making him more aroused, tensed, and excited. The increased epinephrine and norepinephrine would make his heart beat faster and stronger. His blood pressure would have risen. His respiratory rate would increase, all adding to the already increased arousal state he was in. This "build up" of physiological changes gives people that sense of being overwhelmed by anger and seeking a way to escape or end the situation altogether. Cain was experiencing anger from the rejection by God from his own disobedience to the offering he brought to sacrifice. Cain was not right with God. He fully disobeyed, but he had the opportunity to make things right, for his anger had not yet reached the point of sin. God, in His love and compassion, gave Cain a warning as noted in Genesis 4:7 – *"If thou doest well, shalt thou not be accepted? and if thou doest not well, sin lieth at the door. And unto thee shall be his desire, and thou shalt rule over him."* The fact that sin was at the door and had not come in shows that Cain was in grave danger of sinning but had not yet crossed the line.

The intense physiological reaction produced by our adrenal glands can potentially deceive us into thinking that our anger is beyond control, and that we have to give into it. This is another lie. When we find ourselves physiologically overcome, leading to an emotional upheaval, sin is lying at the door. We must master our physiological and emotional upheaval. This is our responsibility. We are not controlled by our adrenal glands nor by the epinephrine and the norepinephrine it produces and releases into our blood system. We are not controlled by the heightened arousal our physical body feels. We are to be controlled by God and His Word. If we are not controlled by God, we will be the worse for it. Some will say, "That is just the way I am." Some even say, "Tempers run in our family." These are poor excuses that many put their trust in.

We should not take anger lightly, nor should we declare it to be our ethnic heritage. Everyone can turn to God and His Word and choose the truth whereby we can control anger. The question that needs to be asked: When does the emotion of anger become sin? God warned Cain, "If thou doest not well" (Genesis 5:7). Cain had the opportunity to offer the proper God-ordained sacrifice. Had he done so, his anger would have been gone and so would have its physical effects. (His countenance would have been lifted up.) When the emotion of anger becomes wrath or rage (thumos) or fleshly hostility (orge), it has become sin according to God's Word.

Anger has become a controlling agent that causes us to behave wrongly. In the case we are discussing, it resulted in Cain murdering his brother, Abel. This act of murder was the end result of Cain's uncontrolled anger. In reality, Cain had murdered Abel in his heart before he carried out the deed with his hands. In Matthew 5:21-22 – *"Ye have heard that it was said by them of old time, Thou shalt not kill; and whosoever shall kill shall be in danger of the judgment: But I say unto you, That whosoever is angry with his brother without a cause shall be in danger of the judgment: and whosoever shall say to his brother,*

Raca, shall be in danger of the council: but whosoever shall say, Thou fool, shall be in danger of hell fire." - Jesus teaches us that the battle has to be won in our hearts (the seat of our emotions, which is part of our soul).

We must maintain control over our emotions. In order to do so, we must assume responsibility for the way we think. The anger is there because we have mentally translated what our physical senses have picked up. God has given us the ability and capacity to choose what we are going to do with the information our senses have picked up and sent to our brains. If we choose God's way, which is the truth, then we will manage properly our emotional responses of anger. The only way to maintain control is to continuously think righteously or in agreement to God and His Word. Anger that leads to unrighteous thoughts and deeds is sinful and destructive. Anger that stimulates us to righteous thoughts and deeds is good. It is what Paul told the Christians in Rome in Romans 12:21 – *"Be not overcome of evil, but overcome evil with good."* However, allowing anger to remain in our hearts is the same thing as letting the sun go down on our wrath, which gives the devil the opportunity to operate in our lives. Ephesians 4:27 – *"Neither give place to the devil."* I Peter 5:8 – *"Be sober, be vigilant; because your adversary the devil, as a roaring lion, walketh about, seeking whom he may devour:"*

Anger results in angry words that grieve the Holy Spirit. Ephesians 4:29-30 – *"Let no corrupt communication proceed out of your mouth, but that which is good to the use of edifying, that it may minister grace unto the hearers. And grieve not the holy Spirit of God, whereby ye are sealed unto the day of redemption."* It deteriorates into *"bitterness, and wrath, and anger"* along with *"all malice"* (Ephesians 4:31).

To end this battle for our minds (a part of our soul), we must meditate on God's Word. All thoughts that step into the door of our minds must be run through the filter of God's Word. The thoughts that would go contrary to God and His Word must be cast down, and the thoughts that are in line with

God and His Word must be captivated. II Corinthians 10:5 – *"Casting down imaginations, and every high thing that exalteth itself against the knowledge of God, and bringing into captivity every thought to the obedience of Christ;"* In other words, if what we are thinking is not in line with God and His Word, we must not set our minds to it. Choose, rather, to think on things that are true, right, pure, honorable, and so on. Philippians 4:8 – *"Finally, brethren, whatsoever things are true, whatsoever things are honest, whatsoever things are just, whatsoever things are pure, whatsoever things are lovely, whatsoever things are of good report; if there be any virtue, and if there be any praise, think on these things."*

---

nger

CHAPTER FOUR:
HIDDEN NEEDS

Brian was a great pastor. If you ever met him, you would not think that he had an underlying problem with anger. But, like many of us, he had learned to hide it very effectively. He had channeled his anger into a driven work ethic that had served him well in the pastorate. As he approached his twentieth year of pastoring his church and you looked deep into his life, you would have seen that his family was falling apart. Even though he was the spiritual leader of a church, his own spiritual life was weak. His wife had become bitter, and Brian was having a difficult time maintaining an intimate, dynamic relationship with Jesus Christ.

Brian saw that all the things that were precious to him were on the verge of collapsing and sought out advice and counsel. During one of these counseling sessions, it was noted that Brian's parents were very distant and very unsupportive of Brian and his desire and call to be in the ministry. This made Brian angry. Instead of facing his anger, he channeled that energy into his ministry, which, on the surface, looked quite successful; but in actuality, he had an impoverished soul. Brian was insecure in a lot of ways. He had come to view God like his parents – distant and uninterested. Through counseling, he was able to see that God, his Father, is the Father he always needed and wanted. Brian forgave his parents, and he came to realize that he no longer needed to perform to impress God. He came to realize that God's love was and is unconditional. I am happy to say that Brian just celebrated his twenty-seventh anniversary at the same church, and his church is growing and thriving as well as his marriage and family.

As Brian grew up, we see that he had many unmet needs in his life. These unmet needs resulted in much pain as well as anger. Most, if not all of us, have experienced this in one way or another. But, this is not how God intended us to be. When Adam and Eve lived in the garden, every need they had was perfectly met by God. They experienced a deep sense of significance because they had been given dominion over all the earth. Genesis 1:28 – *"And God blessed them, and God said unto them, Be fruitful, and multiply, and replenish the earth, and subdue it: and have dominion over the fish of the sea, and over the fowl of the air, and over every living thing that moveth upon the earth."* They also felt secure because God the Father had provided for all their needs. Likewise, they felt accepted by one another because *"they were both naked, the man and his wife, and were not ashamed"* (Genesis 2:25). They also had joy and intimacy because both had an intimate, dynamic love relationship with Jesus Christ. As well, they had dignity because they were created in the image of God. Genesis 1:26-27 – *"And God said, Let us make man in our image, after our likeness: and let them have dominion over the fish of the sea, and over the fowl of the air, and over the cattle, and over all the earth, and over every creeping thing that creepeth upon the earth. So God created man in his own image, in the image of God created he him; male and female created he them."*

Because all their needs were met, they experienced no frustration or injustice; thus, there was no anger. Adam and Eve lived in perfect peace with God and each other. When Adam and Eve sinned, paradise was shattered. Sin had entered into their world, and now life was different. Adam and Eve immediately felt fear, shame, and guilt. They attempted to cover their own physical nakedness with fig leaves and then foolishly attempted to hide from the very presence of God. Genesis 3:7-8 – *"And the eyes of them both were opened, and they knew that they were naked; and they sewed fig leaves together, and made themselves aprons. And they heard the voice of the LORD God walking in the garden in the cool of the day: and Adam and his wife hid themselves from the presence of the LORD God amongst the trees of the garden. "* Adam and Eve experienced spiritual death when their sin separated them from God. Because of their sin, they and their descendants would have to experience every kind of physical and emotional distress that leads to physical death. As a result of the sin of Adam and Eve, we have all entered this world physically alive but spiritually dead.

In our physical life, we are all descendants of Adam and Eve. Therefore, you could say that apart from Jesus Christ we are all a part of Adam's family. We can say that we are in Adam. I Corinthians 15:22 – *"For as in Adam all die, even so in Christ shall all be made alive."* Paul's words in Ephesians 2:1-3 provide a precise and accurate description of our condition apart from Christ – *"And you hath he quickened, who were dead in trespasses and sins; Wherein in time past ye walked according to the course of this world, according to the prince of the power of the air, the spirit that now worketh in the children of disobedience: Among whom also we all had our conversation in times past in the lusts of our flesh, fulfilling the desires of the flesh and of the mind; and were by nature the children of wrath, even as others."*

Without Jesus Christ in our lives we have no alternative but to be dominated by the world, the flesh, and the devil. Without Christ as our Savior our body can physically function together with our soul (mind, will, and emotions), but we are spiritually dead; we are cut off from God. There is no relationship or fellowship with God whatsoever. Because we have no relationship, thus, no fellowship with God, we obviously learn to live our lives separate or independent from God. During these years when we live apart from God, we develop certain mindsets, which are similar to what psychologists call defense mechanism or coping skills. We have to learn how to cope, succeed, and survive with only our limited strengths and resources. Most of our coping skills we learn from within our own homes as well as the friends we have, the schools we attend, and even the churches we attend.

We must realize two individuals can be raised in a very similar environment but can choose to respond differently; thus, they can develop totally different coping skills. Traumatic experiences that we live through can also help shape our defense mechanisms or coping skills. In fact, if we live through a traumatic experience, then now as an adult we see someone else going through the same traumatic experience, we will probably react in an angry way. Traumas in our childhood keep us in bondage to the lies we have believed as a result of such experiences. This is why the Bible says in John 8:32, *"the truth shall make you free."*

You see, when you went through that traumatic experience, you processed in your mind what was happening and then you chose how to respond to that traumatic event. How you chose to respond then established a belief about that circumstance and even about people in general. If it was an experience where you felt unloved and unwanted, you may have established a belief that no one loves you and no one wants you, including God. If you grew up constantly having to perform to feel accepted, you probably developed a coping mechanism whereby, even today, you feel you must perform to be accepted, even by God. With all of these defense mechanisms and coping skills that we develop and live our lives without Jesus Christ, we then must adopt certain ways of defending ourselves, such as blaming others, lying, rationalizing, denying, withdrawing, fighting, and so on. Many individuals will hold on to their anger which they falsely believe will protect them from some future abuse. No matter how hard we try we cannot, by our own effort and merit, regain what was lost by Adam and Eve in paradise. We cannot, by our own effort and merit, obtain that sense of dignity, joy, security, acceptance, and significance that they had in paradise. When you think about it, this is really what we are all desiring and searching for. Even our best efforts will fail, and we will fall short of obtaining what was lost in paradise. As we continue to live a life apart from Christ, we will be hopelessly tainted by our past and our sins because we are separated from God. If that makes us angry, then consider Paul's words in Titus 1:15-16 – *"Unto the pure all things are pure: but unto them that are defiled and unbelieving is nothing pure; but even their mind and conscience is defiled. They profess that they know God; but in works they deny him, being abominable, and disobedient, and unto every good work reprobate.*" Apart from the Lord Jesus Christ, we have no choice but to live according to our own flesh.

Although there is never any excuse for living in sin and selfishness, the truth of the matter is that someone who rejects Christ as Savior has no other alternative. That individual must live their life by their own defense mechanism and coping skills or give up on life totally, which, unfortunately, many people do. When we are born physically, we are products of our mother and father's genetic makeup. Many times, because of faulty chromosomes or mutations that occur during the child's development, birth defects can occur. All of us, to an extent, were born with a birth defect, which is sinful and idolatress to its very core. It is sinful because it is a life that is lived independent of God's presence and power. It is idolatrous because it places us at the center of our lives instead of the Lord Jesus Christ. The Apostle Paul definitively hits the nail on the head in Romans 8:5-8 – "*For they that are after the flesh do mind the things of the flesh; but they that are after the Spirit the things of the Spirit. For to be carnally minded is death; but to be spiritually minded is life and peace. Because the carnal mind is enmity against God: for it is not subject to the law of God, neither indeed can be. So then they that are in the flesh cannot please God.*" We, thus, are very selfish individuals.

The main goal of our flesh is to preserve itself, protect itself, and provide for itself; thus, it is extremely selfish. Our flesh is self-protective, self-reliant, self-promoting, and self-serving. The flesh is continually on the lookout for the threat of angry conflict with others. Why would our flesh be on the lookout for the threat of angry conflict of others? It is because you have one self-protective, self-reliant, self-promoting, and self-serving individual encountering others of the same sort. Angry conflicts are unavoidable in this setting. When I am trying to get my own needs met doing things my way, and you stand in my way, my fleshly defense mechanism and coping skills that I have developed from the past will tell me to become threatening and angry so that I may get my way. James speaks of it like this: *"From whence come wars and fightings among you? come they not hence, even of your lusts that war in your members? Ye lust, and have not: ye kill, and desire to have, and cannot obtain: ye fight and war, yet ye have not, because ye ask not. Ye ask, and receive not, because ye ask amiss, that ye may consume it upon your lusts"* (James 4:1-3).

A person who does not have Jesus Christ as their Savior can only live according to their own fleshly nature. But, when we come to know Jesus Christ as our Savior, we are born into the family of God, become the children of God, and we have experienced a supernatural transformation. Paul tells us about this supernatural transformation in II Corinthians 5:17 – *"Therefore if any man be in Christ, he is a new creature: old things are passed away; behold, all things are become new."* As children of God, we are no longer simply a product of our past experiences with learned defense mechanisms and coping skills. We are now a product of the finished work of Jesus Christ on the cross, His glorious resurrection, and the power of the resurrected life. Because we are children of God and have experienced this supernatural transformation, we no longer have to live for ourselves, but we can now live for the Lord Jesus Christ, the One who died and rose again for our justification. II Corinthians 5:15 – *"And that he died for all, that they which live should not henceforth live unto themselves, but unto him which died for them, and rose again."*

The Holy Spirit of God now resides within us making us the temple of God. The Holy Sprit of God who now lives within us wants to empower us so that we may walk in the spirit and not in the flesh. The Holy Spirit of God will empower us to live in Christ. I Corinthians 6:19 – *"What? know ye not that your body is the temple of the Holy Ghost which is in you, which ye have of God, and ye are not your own?"* Romans 6:4 – *"Therefore we are buried with him by baptism into death: that like as Christ was raised up from the dead by the glory of the Father, even so we also should walk in newness of life."* Romans 8:13 – *"For if ye live after the flesh, ye shall die: but if ye through the Spirit do mortify the deeds of the body, ye shall live."* Now that we are new creatures in Christ, why do we still feel and think much the same way as we did prior to our salvation? Why do I still struggle with my bitterness, unforgiveness, selfishness, and angry attitude?

The answer is quite clear. All of the defense mechanisms and all of the coping skills that we learned from our past lives and past experiences are still a part of our mind. When we receive Jesus Christ as our Savior, God does not wipe our minds clear, but He commands us to renew our minds as Paul writes about in Romans 12:2 – *"And be not conformed to this world: but be ye transformed by the renewing of your mind, that ye may prove what is that good, and acceptable, and perfect, will of God."* If we continue to live the same way we lived before we knew Jesus Christ as our Savior, we will continue to be conformed to this world. Now that we are children of God through the Lord Jesus Christ we have the mind of Christ available to us. I Corinthians 2:16 – *"For who hath known the mind of the Lord, that he may instruct him? But we have the mind of Christ."* We also have the Holy Spirit within us Who will guide us into all truth. This does not happen instantly at the time of salvation, but we must choose to allow our minds to be renewed moment by moment by the truth of God's Word.

As we allow our minds to be renewed moment by moment through the truth of God's Word, our old defense mechanisms and our old coping skills will slowly fade away. You see, initially we lived life for ourselves. We were, as we mentioned earlier, extremely selfish. Before we came to Jesus Christ, we, in essence, were our own god, and we became angry at other people because we felt they did not treat us the way we deserved to be treated. Now, we are believers in the Lord Jesus Christ, and we have come to find out that life is not about us but about God the Father and His glory and honor. We have also found out that we were made to worship Him. With all of this transpiring in our lives, the Holy Spirit will manifest those ungodly defense mechanisms and coping skills. The Holy

Spirit will expose the anger that lives deep within us. What we once considered a normal part of life, God has now exposed it for what it is and that is sin. The Holy Spirit will not stop there. He will empower us to confess and forsake those sins, so that He might live through us.

As you come to this point in the book, you may say, "I have never accepted Jesus Christ as my Savior." "I am not a child of God." Then, today is the day you need to come to Jesus Christ for salvation. The Bible says, *"now is the accepted time; behold, now is the day of salvation"* (II Corinthians 6:2). Jesus Christ became *"sin for us, who knew no sin; that we might be made the righteousness of God in him"* (II Corinthians 5:21). Are you willing to make the great exchange – your sin for the righteousness of Jesus Christ? Will you now receive the free gift of God which is eternal life in the Lord Jesus Christ, or will you continue in your sin and suffer the wages of sin which is death and hell? Romans 6:23 – *"For the wages of sin is death; but the gift of God is eternal life through Jesus Christ our Lord."* If you, right now, find your heart hungry for God and want to become one of His children and seek His forgiveness and His righteousness and begin a new life in Him, then I encourage you to pray with me:

Dear Heavenly Father, I have sinned against You. I have trusted in my own effort and my own works which I know can never gain me Heaven. I am a sinner, and I have fallen short of Your glory. I now realize and understand that Jesus Christ, Your Son, God in the flesh, came to earth and lived a perfect life, died on the cross, shed His blood, was buried, and rose again three days later in order to pay for my sin. I know I cannot save myself; only Jesus Christ can save me. I now repent of my sin and ask the Lord Jesus Christ to be my Savior. I realize that this gift from You is free and undeserving but is made available to me by Your grace. Thank You, Jesus, for making me a child of God and a new creation in You. In Jesus' Name I pray, Amen.

As children of God, we now have the very power of God

within us through the Holy Spirit to empower us to live in a way that is worthy of our calling. Ephesians 4:1 – *"I therefore, the prisoner of the Lord, beseech you that ye walk worthy of the vocation wherewith ye are called..."* When the Apostle Paul wrote, *"Now unto him that is able to do exceeding abundantly above all that we ask or think, according to the power that worketh in us"* (Ephesians 4:20), he was describing the power that the Holy Spirit of God gives to us. God can change your life! Please! Do not doubt God's ability to change your life. Do not become skeptical about God's ability. Take courage in this fact that God can take your anger and turn it into gentleness and kindness. There are those who, upon receiving Jesus Christ as their Savior, will have a miraculous deliverance from their anger and rage. But, with most children of God, it will take time for their minds to be renewed. It will take time for those old defense mechanisms and coping skills to be done away with and replaced with Godly thoughts and actions.

We should take comfort that the bondage that we once had to anger does not have to follow us for the rest of our lives. For those that are struggling with controlling anger in your life, please take great hope from what Paul tells us in II Corinthians 10:3-5 – *"For though we walk in the flesh, we do not war after the flesh: (For the weapons of our warfare are not carnal, but mighty through God to the pulling down of strong holds;) Casting down imaginations, and every high thing that exalteth itself against the knowledge of God, and bringing into captivity every thought to the obedience of Christ;"*

As we discussed earlier in this chapter, we must remember that those ungodly defense mechanisms and coping skills that make us act contrary to God's Word are deeply ingrained in us. They are a thought process within our minds. It has been placed there through traumatic experiences that we have lived through. Living by these defense mechanisms and coping skills is like driving a bicycle in a rut. It does not take much thought and effort; but if you desire to ride the bike outside of that rut, you will meet up with resistance. However, the Holy Spirit of God will give you the power to break free from that rut or, in this case, those ungodly defense mechanisms and coping skills. The good news is that no matter how powerful these defense mechanisms and coping skills are, God's power is greater. Parts of our personality that we thought would not and could not ever change can be truly transformed by the power of the Lord Jesus Christ. If you find yourself enslaved to anger and rage, you can be made free. Instead of being led by your anger and rage, you can be guided *"in the paths of righteousness for his name's sake"* (Psalm 23:3).

As we close this chapter, please realize that Jesus Christ can meet every need that you have and can give you freedom over your anger.

CHAPTER FIVE:
DEFENSE MECHANISM & COPING SKILL MANIFESTATIONS

"Evangelist D. L. Moody was one of the greatest preachers of the nineteenth century, but he had a sharp temper that he learned to control – usually. One evening, Moody was conducting two evangelistic services back to back. After the first service, as Mr. Moody was standing near the door greeting the new crowd, a man approached him and delivered a highly-offensive insult of some sort. Moody never told what the insult was, but it must have been contemptible; for in a sudden fit of anger, Moody shoved the man and sent him tumbling down a short flight of steps."

"The man was not badly harmed, but Moody's friends wondered how the evangelist could possibly preach at the second service. An observer said, 'When I saw Moody give way to his temper, I said to myself, the meeting is killed. The large number who saw the whole thing would hardly be in condition to be influenced by anything more Mr. Moody can say tonight.' "

"But, Moody stood up, called the meeting to order, and with a trembling voice spoke these words: Friends, before beginning tonight, I want to confess that I yielded just now to my temper out in the hall and have done wrong. Just as I was coming in here tonight, I lost my temper with a man, and I want to confess my wrong before you all. If that man is present here whom I thrust away from me in anger, I want to ask his forgiveness and God's. Let us pray. Instead of being a lost cause, the meeting seemed unusually touched that night with many people deeply and internally impressed with the Gospel." *[William R. Moody, The Life of Dwight L. Moody, Murfreesboro, TN, Sword of the Lord Publishers, pgs. 110-111]*

We have all, growing up, developed at least one defense mechanism of coping skill which has to do with anger. We may be very aware of those defense mechanisms or coping skills that deal in one way or another with anger, but we might also be having success as we find ourselves being liberated from those angry attitudes by the Holy Spirit of God just like Dwight Moody did that evening he preached as discussed above. But, on the other hand, there are many people who are unaware of their own defense mechanisms and coping skills that have, as a part, anger. Many of these people have come to the conclusion that this is who they are, and others are going to have to deal with it, and others will have to learn to live with it as well. This is a spectrum. At one end, some people are being liberated from their ungodly defense mechanisms and coping skills through the Holy Spirit of God. At the other end of the spectrum are those that are telling others to deal with it and live with it because this is the way they have been and always will be. So, you have the two opposite poles of this spectrum, but most people will find themselves somewhere in between. Many individuals realize that their defense mechanisms and coping skills are not right according to the Word of God, but they truly lack insight on what to do about it. Before we can experience the transforming of God in tearing down these defense mechanisms and coping skills, we first need to understand how these defense mechanisms and coping skills became a reality in our lives.

In this chapter, I would like to discuss some of the more **common manifestations** of these **defense mechanisms** and **coping skills** with the desire that it will provide a helpful evaluation of your soul.

1.   **Individuals that try to stay away from anger**

These individuals do not like anger. For them, anger means losing control, or they may look at it as letting the monster out that lives inside of them. Therefore, they end up hiding their anger. These individuals will be those that will try to keep the peace at all cost. They feel very uncomfortable around anger, and they will generally accommodate and appease whenever possible. If they are not able to accommodate and appease, they find themselves exiting the situation lest anger be manifested. This group of people is basically out of touch with their emotions. Some will go as far as saying that they do not have any anger in their lives. This is not true! All of us at certain times in our lives are going to deal with this emotion of anger. By believing that we do not have anger in our lives, we believe another lie from the devil. In the case of all bondage, the individual must renounce the lie that he or she has believed and choose the truth. We do have anger, and we need to give it over to the Lord Jesus Christ through the empowering of the Holy Spirit of God.

Are you an individual that tries to hide from anger? Have you had the feeling of guilt when you have experienced just a touch of anger? Have you believed that good Christians don't get angry? Have you ever found yourself getting angry at yourself for not being more assertive? Have you hung up the phone and kicked yourself for having donated money to a cause you had no intention of doing so? Please realize that those individuals that try to hide from anger are using a defense mechanism or a coping skill that has a fear of anger, a fear of confrontation, a fear of disapproval, and a fear of rejection. If the Holy Spirit is prompting you to realize you are an individual that tries to avoid anger or hide from anger, please do not get discouraged. Jesus Christ is here to make you free so that you can be *"angry and sin not"* (Ephesians 4:26).

2.   Individuals that let anger out at the drop of a hat

This is the other end of the spectrum as compared to number one above. These individuals express anger too freely and are then very capable of doing great harm to others. Because this group can cause such devastation, I would like to examine this defense mechanism or coping skill more in depth.

First, let me give you an *illustration*: I am a young man that is currently working through the Reformers Unanimous curriculum with the assistance of my RU director as well as my pastor who has taking a very active role in my recovery. God has worked in so many areas of my life so far, and I have experienced, in many facets of my life, freedom through the Lord Jesus Christ. I have always had a quick temper, easy to flare up and am very quick to let my anger out. I know that my anger has scared other people, but being honest, it has also scared me at times. What generally happens in my life is that I allow all of the stress and frustration to continue to build and build up and then something insignificant will happen and push the flood gates open and out comes my anger. When the dust clears, I feel humbled, disillusioned, and empty. I have tried other anger management programs, and they teach avoidance of the situation as the coping mechanism. The anger avoidance method that they teach is just a worldly means of dealing with the situation. If God is softly speaking to you about this avoidance of anger in your life, then thank the Lord, for He is opening your eyes to reality. Do not get discouraged by the fact that you lie in this category, for we know that Jesus can make you free. With Jesus making us free, we, then, through the power of the Holy Spirit of God, can be *"angry and sin not"* (Ephesians 4:26).

3. Individuals that express anger at any given time

On one end of the spectrum you have those who avoid anger at almost any cost. At the other end of the spectrum are those who exhibit angry behavior quite frequently in their lives. These individuals express anger so freely and generally do great damage to other people. This type of anger expression deserves our close look into it.

Those that very easily demonstrate their anger can be likened unto hurricanes. With any hurricane, there is always the threat of damage. Some hurricanes may cause minimal damage while others cause massive destruction. Regardless of the level of the hurricane that is out there, there is always going to be some type of damage associated with it. This is like the individuals that express anger all too easily. Damage always follows! These individuals live in a constant state of agitation or in a constant state of being stirred up and ready to explode. These people are brewing all day long in their anger, and that is why they erupt at the slightest provocation. They do not need time to warm up to anger like most of the general population needs. They are already angry, and they are ready to cause damage at any time. Those that have an undercurrent of anger in their lives may say that they are trying to meet their God-given goals. In attempting to reach their God-given goals, they may use anger to stimulate or motivate people so that the goals are met. However, if someone has been given a goal to reach by God, it does not give them a license to angrily control or trample the people under them. God is certainly interested in achieving goals but never at the expense of others. James encourages us in this matter. James 1:19-20 – *"Wherefore, my beloved brethren, let every man be swift to hear, slow to speak, slow to wrath: For the wrath of man worketh not the righteousness of God."*

Many good Christians have a Godly task given to them to complete. They are given a group of people to help them complete that task in a timely fashion. All too often, the leader will become impatient and insensitive to the people who are under them. They end up stepping on many toes as they crusade forward to accomplish their task. These individuals need to daily meditate upon I Corinthians 13:13 – *"And now abideth faith, hope, charity, these three; but the greatest of these is charity."* The Lord Jesus Christ is telling us through the Apostle Paul that in our efforts to complete the God-given tasks that are before us, we must agape love the people under us. In doing so, this is the greatest motivator in the world.

At this juncture of the book, a warning needs to be given to Christian leaders. Those that are in leadership positions within the local church will have a stricter judgment according to

James 3:1 – *"My brethren, be not many masters, knowing that we shall receive the greater condemnation."* So, we must be careful that as we go about attempting to meet our God-given tasks and goals, meeting our budgets, or building a bigger and better worship center that we do not go about whipping those sheep under our care. According to Numbers 12:3, Moses was the meekest man on earth; and yet, he was also a man given to several angry outbursts. *"(Now the man Moses was very meek, above all the men which were upon the face of the earth.)"* In Numbers, chapter 20, there is recorded one instance where Moses made a terrible mistake in regards to his anger. Numbers 20:7-12 – *"And the LORD spake unto Moses, saying, Take the rod, and gather thou the assembly together, thou, and Aaron thy brother, and speak ye unto the rock before their eyes; and it shall give forth his water, and thou shalt bring forth to them water out of the rock: so thou shalt give the congregation and their beasts drink. And Moses took the rod from before the LORD, as he commanded him. And Moses and Aaron gathered the congregation together before the rock, and he said unto them, Hear now, ye rebels; must we fetch you water out of this rock? And Moses lifted up his hand, and with his rod he smote the rock twice: and the water came out abundantly, and the congregation drank, and their beasts also. And the LORD spake unto Moses and Aaron, Because ye believed me not, to sanctify me in the eyes of the children of Israel, therefore ye shall not bring this congregation into the land which I have given them."* This passage holds a strong warning for leaders within the local church today. God is loving and kind and will take care of His people even when His leaders fail. But, if we try to control God's people in anger, we may find the Lord rising up against us and opposing the very goals He once gave us. In the end, like it was with Moses, we may only gaze with longing eyes upon the dreams we once drove so mightily to fulfill.

Some individuals that are basically stewing in anger all the time and can easily explode at any time are like this because of painful experiences in their lives. Those individuals who have suffered neglect and abuse in their earlier lives and have not had the opportunity to release their anger can become very angry, bitter people. These people generally will not be forgiving people, but they will keep the proverbial list of all those who have hurt them. These people that are unforgiving and, thus, have become angry, bitter people must heed the warning given to them in Matthew 18:34 – *"And his lord was wroth, and delivered him to the tormentors, till he should pay all that was due unto him."* These people are convinced that others are out to get them. They will preemptively lash out in anger hurting others before they can be hurt. These people are hurting deeply, and they need our love and forgiveness so that their wounds may start to heal. What will happen in many cases as others try to help them and befriend them is that they will drive away those that are trying to help. They, in a sense, sabotage these relationships with other people that are trying to help them. They sabotage these relationships because they feel if they let people too close to them, they will be more vulnerable to hurt and rejection. In actuality, they are choking off the flow of life-giving love from God and others.

There is another group that is closely associated with those that have suffered neglect and abuse in the past, and those are the individuals that have an enormous amount of shame in their lives. They feel unloved and unworthy. They also feel shameful and dirty. Therefore, they will use anger towards the rest of the world in the attempt to keep them at a safe, emotional distance. You see, they feel that it is too risky to allow other people to get too close in a relationship. They feel if other people get too close they may discover the skeletons in their closets and be as repulsed as they are by what they see. So, again, they use anger formulated out of self-loathing, and they use it to ward off those that are getting way too close to them and their buried pain of past sins and shame.

There is another group of individuals who have a heightened level of anger in their lives and are ready to explode at any moment, and they are the people in this world who are literally addicted to anger. These people get a feeling of euphoria, or they get a high, from the surge of anger in their bodies. When someone has an anger outburst, the adrenal glands pump more epinephrine and norepinephrine into the person's blood system. This increase of epinephrine and norepinephrine in to the person's blood system makes their heart beat faster, there is increased breathing, their muscles become tense, and there is a dumping of dopamine into the front part of the brain; all of this causing the euphoria or high that is associated with anger. To these individuals, anger is like injecting excitement into a dull day. But, there is a condition called tolerance. Tolerance demands more and more of the drug to get the desired high. Tolerance also occurs in this phenomenon of anger addiction. It takes more anger and more intensive anger for the individual to get the desired high or euphoria from their angry outburst. The result of this can truly be deadly in the home, on the road, or elsewhere.

4.   Individuals that use anger to exploit others

This person enjoys the power that comes from anger and believes that by using anger, or the potential outburst of anger, they gain power over other individuals. These individuals tend to get an emotional rush from their anger. They get this emotional rush by creating fear in others and making others give them what they want. Those that use anger to exploit others are basically grown-up little children that are, in essence, throwing temper tantrums. Probability states that they were permitted to throw temper tantrums as a child. This stronghold was firmly established in their younger age, and now it has taken a more sophisticated facade in their adult years.

5.   Individuals that necessarily don't show anger on the outside but certainly have anger on the inside.

All the while these individuals look calm on the outside, but they are calculating revenge on the inside. This type of person lives by the motto: I don't get mad, I get even! In actuality, this person does both.

The Bible contains several examples of this kind of stronghold in a person's life.

The first example is with King David's son, Absalom, who waited two full years after his half-brother, Amnon, raped his sister, Tamar, to carry out his plan of revenge on him. The festering anger inside of Absalom showed up when he plotted to overthrow the throne of his father, David. After three years in exile following the murder of Amnon, King David permitted Absalom to come back to Jerusalem to live. However, David refused to see him for two more years even though they lived just a few minutes from each other. Absalom's resentment over this went to the deepest part of his being. Absalom secretly took revenge against his father and stole the hearts of the people away from him. II Samuel 15:6 – *"And on this manner did Absalom to all Israel that came to the king for judgment: so Absalom stole the hearts of the men of Israel."* Absalom was attempting to usurp his father's throne. II Samuel 15:10 – *"But Absalom sent spies throughout all the tribes of Israel, saying, As soon as ye hear the sound of the trumpet, then ye shall say, Absalom reigneth in Hebron."* His disdain for his father was further evidenced by his sleeping with David's concubines. II Samuel 16:22 – *"So they spread Absalom a tent upon the top of the house; and Absalom went in unto his father's concubines in the sight of all Israel."*

Another vivid illustration found in the Bible that demonstrates this seething revenge is Esau and Jacob. Esau was the older twin brother of Jacob. He displayed in his heart the calculating revenge that this type of person will have. Esau had this calculating revenge in response to Jacob's deceitful theft of their father's (Isaac) blessing. Genesis 27:41 tells the story – *"And Esau hated Jacob because of the blessing wherewith his father blessed him: and Esau said in his heart, The days of mourning for my father are at hand; then will I slay my brother Jacob."* Fortunately, for both brothers, the story had a very happy ending. Jacob escaped from Esau, and the two were eventually reconciled many years later. Esau never took the revenge he first threatened.

In the upcoming chapter on forgiveness, we will explain why taking revenge is useless and wrong. For now, though, let us look at Romans 12:17-21 to renew our minds to this truth.

"Recompense to no man evil for evil. Provide things honest in the sight of all men. If it be possible, as much as lieth in you, live peaceably with all men. Dearly beloved, avenge not yourselves, but rather give place unto wrath: for it is written, Vengeance is mine; I will repay, saith the Lord. Therefore if thine enemy hunger, feed him; if he thirst, give him drink: for in so doing thou shalt heap coals of fire on his head. Be not overcome of evil, but overcome evil with good."

6. Individuals are not the scariest to be with or live with, but they are probably the most annoying people to be around

These individuals exhibit the most annoying anger style of all those we have talked about so far and will talk about. They are like a persistent bug on a hot summer night that continues to pick at you. These individuals seem to always be buzzing around with a truckload of complaints. They gripe and complain; in fact, they only appear to be happy when they are unhappy. If things are going well, these individuals will quickly recall a time when things were not. They always think that bad times lie just ahead. No amount of rational argument will keep these individuals quiet for long nor improve their ungodly dispositions. The reason behind this is that these individuals feel life has dealt them bad hands. Whether they are disgruntled at God, others, or themselves, they are angry people. Somewhere in the past, they were deeply hurt, and in many cases, given up hope expecting the worst to transpire. Angry, gripping pessimism becomes their shield against further pain. Apart from genuine repentance toward God and those who have been giving them a "raw" deal, these individuals worsen with age.

Years of functioning in this self-protective mode will most likely produce a cynical, sarcastic, bitter person. Unable to truly enjoy life or experience joy for long, this person feels justified in their anger and their pessimistic view of life. In fact, he or she would call themselves a realest at times, feeling superior to those with a more shallow, optimistic view of life.

7. **Individuals who are critical in every aspect of their lives.**

These individuals are struggling to live up to unrealistic and unkind personal standards and expectations. Since they cannot meet these standards, they feel like they have failed. The ironic thing about these individuals is that the rest of the world is amazed at how much they accomplish and how well they do it. These individuals battle with shame and self-loathing even as they are driven to do things better, faster, harder, and smarter. They are unable to quiet the angry task master that is inside of their heads. Therefore, they pour out their venom on those around them. The unfortunate victims may be spouses, children, employees, or even co-workers in the local church. These individuals are capable of uttering cruel, cutting, and destructive words. Motives are judged. Behaviors are critiqued. Successes are demeaned. Failures magnify a tragic loss situation.

8. **Individuals who are known as the classic, passive aggressive**

The passive aggressive person despises what to do. They hate being bothered, directed, or guided by anyone else. They just want to be left alone, and they are upset with anyone who disturbs the peace. When you look deep into this person's life, what you will find is that they need to have control with the least amount of vulnerability. The passive aggressive, in a sense, has a fear of anger as well as confrontation and potential rejection. Therefore, this fear drives the person to an "in and around" rather than a direct approach to expressing anger. They give off this sense of superiority that grows out of having outwitted his or her opponent, giving the passive aggressive the feeling of power. What is the prize for the passive aggressive? It is being left alone while leaving the other person frustrated and worn out.

As we look back at the eight different types of how anger can be expressed in an individual's life, the Lord may be exposing any stronghold that may be in your life. If He has, don't be discouraged. The Lord is bringing these areas of sin to the surface so that you can be free from the bondage of anger.

Please remember, as we have said before, God did not miraculously eradicate all of our strongholds when we came to know Jesus Christ as our Savior. But, He has given us the grace whereby we can be free of their controlling influences. To become free through the Lord Jesus Christ will require a firm commitment to righteousness and a fierce hatred of evil. No casual, half-hearted effort will do.

---

nger

CHAPTER SIX:
GRACE

It was January 14, 1979, and the children's service at Antioch Baptist Church had just concluded. At that time, I was a thirteen-year-old young man that was helping assist the leader of the children's group and keep "law and order" during the children's program. During the teaching of the lesson that day to the children, I was standing in the back listening very intensively. The individual that was teaching the lesson was explaining to the boys and girls how our heart was black in sin and that only through the shed blood of Jesus Christ could our hearts be washed clean or whiter than snow. You see, you must understand that several years previous to this date, I had been struggling with whether or not I knew Jesus Christ as my personal Savior. I doubted this fact and was living a miserable life. But, on January 14, 1979, as that teacher was presenting the simple truth of the Gospel of Jesus Christ to the children, I finally realized that I was a lost sinner in need of salvation. I found myself going out to the main service, and there I walked the aisle meeting the pastor at the front and expressing to him my dilemma. I told him that even though I thought I knew Jesus Christ as my personal Savior, I, in actuality, had not known Him and that this day, by the grace of God, I was proclaiming Jesus Christ as my personal Savior.

That day, I put my sinful life into the hands of a gracious, merciful God. I cannot describe the release that took place at the moment except to say that the crushing load I felt was gone, and the bitter filth of my soul was cleansed instantaneously. I was amazed! When I went home, I was so excited I told everyone what had happened inside of me. What it all meant I did not know at that time, but I knew it was real. I am now approaching my thirty-third Spiritual birthday, and my heart is still full of the reality of the amazing grace of Jesus Christ. The fullness has even matured over the years.

You might ask yourself the question: Why is there a need to discuss grace in a book about anger? The answer is simple. It is only by the grace of God that we have been made new creatures in Christ. We need the presence of Jesus Christ in our lives so that we can be the kind of individual that He created us to be. It is only by the grace of God that we can be free from our past. God doesn't just fix our past; He makes us free from it along with the anger that has festered for years because of neglect and past abuse. By the grace of God, we are transformed by the renewing of our minds. Romans 12:2 – "And be not conformed to this world: but be ye transformed by the renewing of your mind, that ye may prove what is that good, and acceptable, and perfect, will of God."

Maybe you can't recall a time when you did not believe in Jesus Christ as your Savior, so you can be tempted to believe that your salvation was not so dramatic. You may not have been delivered out of the hard-core drug addiction, sexual immorality, or crime. But, you were just as radically changed inside as anyone else who has come to Jesus Christ. Those children that get saved at age three, four, or five are just as in need of the grace of God as was I when I was saved at thirteen. My friends, we are all in need of the grace of God.

Before we really proceed into all that God has done for us, we need to be reminded, again, of how we were without Jesus Christ in our lives. Paul describes our days before salvation like this: Ephesians 2:12 – *"That at that time ye were without Christ, being aliens from the commonwealth of Israel, and strangers from the covenants of promise, having no hope, and without God in the world:"* Whether the lost person senses alienation from God or not, the separation from God is very real. There are many people in our world that have cancer, but they are dangerously ignorant of the cancer because they have no symptoms in their physical bodies. If they do not discover their true condition soon enough, the cancer will take their lives.

God, through Hosea the prophet, cried out saying, *"My people are destroyed for lack of knowledge: because thou hast rejected knowledge, I will also reject thee, that thou shalt be no priest to me: seeing thou hast forgotten the law of thy God, I will also forget thy children"* (Hosea 4:6). Clearly, there is not more perilous ignorance than that of an unbeliever who is unaware of his or her true Spiritual plight. Romans 5:6-8 tells us the truth regarding the human race's critical condition and Christ's cure. *"For when we were yet without strength, in due time Christ died for the ungodly. For scarcely for a righteous man will one die: yet peradventure for a good man some would even dare to die. But God commendeth his love toward us, in that, while we were yet sinners, Christ died for us."* We can see by the Word of God that without Jesus Christ in our lives we were helpless. We were totally incapable of saving ourselves. Also, according to the Word of God, we were not only helpless but ungodly. We were not only Biblically without help and ungodly, but we were sinners by nature. We were twisted and bent toward self-centeredness and evil.

As you read the Bible's description of we who were without Jesus Christ, you can see God's diagnoses of us without Jesus Christ. That is who we are in Adam. It really isn't a pretty picture is it? Isaiah 64:6 says, *"But we are all as an unclean thing, and all our righteousnesses are as filthy rags; and we all do fade as a leaf; and our iniquities, like the wind, have taken us away."*

Notice the first two words in Romans 5:8 – *"**But God** commendeth his love toward us, in that, while we were yet sinners, Christ died for us."* Those two words are "But God." What a short phrase that demonstrates a tremendous amount of hope. In that short phrase we have an awesome message of deliverance. God wanted to do something so awesome, so remarkable that we would never doubt His love toward us again. So, He sent His Son, Jesus Christ, robed in flesh, to live a perfect, sinless life and had Him pay the ultimate price of death for us who are guilty, helpless sinners. He did this so that we could become forgiven sons and daughters of God. In Ephesians 2:3, Paul describes our spiritually dead condition apart from Jesus Christ. *"Among whom also we all had our conversation in times past in the lusts of our flesh, fulfilling the desires of the flesh and of the mind; and were by nature the children of wrath, even as others."* He ends the verse with His prognosis that outside of Jesus Christ we have no hope. We have no hope of saving ourselves. Again, we see these two words in Ephesians 2:4, "But God." *"**But God**, who is rich in mercy, for his great love wherewith he loved us,"*

My friends, Jesus Christ has saved me and brought me out of the water that was too deep for me and took me safely to the side and set me on Himself, the Solid Rock.

In Luke, chapter 15, Jesus gives us the parables of the lost sheep, the lost coin, and the prodigal son. During the time that Jesus gave these parables, the Scribes and Pharisees were surrounding Him and grumbling because they said Jesus received sinners and ate with them. Luke 15:1-2 – *"Then drew near unto him all the publicans and sinners for to hear him. And the Pharisees and scribes murmured, saying, This man receiveth sinners, and eateth with them."* This is the context in which the parables were given.

In the first parable, we find that the shepherd leaves the ninety-nine sheep that stayed with him to go and find the one that strayed. Luke 15:4 – *"What man of you, having an hundred sheep, if he lose one of them, doth not leave the ninety and nine in the wilderness, and go after that which is lost, until he find it?"* When he does go after the stray and finds it, he lays it on his shoulders with exceeding joy, and he calls his family and friends together to rejoice with him because he found his one lost sheep. We find in this story that the shepherd's love for the one lost sheep was so intense that it never occurred to him not to look for it. When he looked for it, praise God, he found it! In a similar situation, we find a woman who lost one of her ten coins. She lit a lamp and went through the house very carefully searching for this lost coin. Luke 15:8 – *"Either what woman having ten pieces of silver, if she lose one piece, doth not light a candle, and sweep the house, and seek diligently till she find it?"* She finally found the lost coin, and she also called her family and friends together to rejoice with her that she had found the lost coin. Finally, in Luke 15, we find a father with a broken heart. He had given his prodigal son the freedom to leave, but the father kept his eye on the road which led back to home watching and waiting for his son to return. Luke 15:12-13 – *"And the younger of them said to his father, Father, give me the portion of goods that falleth to me. And he divided unto them his living. And not many days after the younger son gathered all together, and took his journey into a far country, and there wasted his substance with riotous living."* We must consider the father's reaction when the son did return. Let us look at the words of Jesus and allow them to impact us today. Luke 15:20-24 – *"And he arose, and came to his father. But when he was yet a great way off, his father saw him, and had compassion, and ran, and fell on his neck, and kissed him. And the son said unto him, Father, I have sinned against heaven, and in thy sight, and am no more worthy to be called thy son. But the father said to his servants, Bring forth the best robe, and put it on him; and put a ring on his hand, and shoes on his feet: And bring hither the fatted calf, and kill it; and let us eat, and be merry: For this my son was dead, and is alive again; he was lost, and is found. And they began to be merry."* God gave us these parables so that we can acknowledge how much God loves lost people. We also are able to observe in these parables that lost people matter so much to God that it warrants an all-out search to find them. Lastly, when one lost person receives the Lord, there is an incredible celebration in Heaven.

For a moment, put yourself in the place of the prodigal son. Can you imagine wasting all of the good things God has given you? You are wasting your life in sin desperately trying to survive. Can you imagine that you finally came to your senses and repented as you run back to the Father? You are riddled with guilt for what you have done. You are filled with shame for what you've become. Can you hear yourself confessing your sin to your Heavenly Father? But, our Heavenly Father pours gracious words out of His mouth. Picture our Heavenly Father running towards you to embrace you and not wanting to miss one second of fellowship with you. As you look into His eyes, you can see the intense compassion and deep love (agape love) that He has for you. You feel His strong, gracious embrace, and you partake of His joy as He kisses you upon your cheek. As the Heavenly Father does all of this to you, you can then start to feel your dignity and sense of worth being restored. The Heavenly Father quickly refuses your request to be made a servant. He acknowledges to you that you are not His servant but His child. Our Heavenly Father has no thought in His heart that we would be anything but His child. As the Heavenly Father puts the robe and ring of honor on you and puts the sandals upon your dusty feet, can you imagine what gratitude you would have for your Heavenly Father? You notice the feast that has been prepared in your honor. You see your family and friends sitting around the table, realizing that all of this is for you because you are a child of God. Does the above circumstance seem hard for you to imagine? Does it somehow seem beneath God to revel and celebrate with such joy? This is our Heavenly Father celebrating His free gift of love and kindness – from death to life, from lost to found, from disgrace to grace.

The grace of God cannot but sweep us off our feet with shear wonder and joy. The tragedy for so many children of God, however, is that in their own perception their Savior has become their judge. They once knew grace, and now they experience guilt. They once enjoyed the feast of freedom of forgiveness; but now, they labor among a yoke of slavery to the law seeking desperately to please a seemingly unpleasable God. In their guilt, they find themselves angry with God, themselves, church and even preachers. Who would not be angry? After all, what is more frustrating than being expected to do the impossible? What we need to do is to try and make sense out of all of this.

I would like to assume that you are a child of God, and you

have placed your faith in the Lord Jesus Christ as your Savior. Now, I would like for you to think, what would be the first words out of the mouth of Jesus if He were to appear to you right now? Many believe that He would say, "Shape up or ship out!" Others might think He would say, "Try harder!" Others would think He would say, "What's wrong with you? Can't you get it?" I don't want to put words into God's mouth, but I believe that Jesus would not say any of the above. I believe Jesus would probably say something like this: "Grace and peace to you from God our Father." This phrase is seen in fifteen of the New Testament letters to the churches and to specific individuals. This is not some typical, ordinary type of greeting; but it is a blessing from God to remind those that would read the letter about their right-standing before their Heavenly Father. They were standing before their Heavenly Father by His grace and with His peace and nothing could change that. What an encouragement to know that despite sins in their midst and trials and perils in their lives, they were forgiven, accepted, and affirmed completely, irrevocably, and eternally. Have you ever thought why there is such an intense battle in our minds to believe that truth? I believe that it is because our enemy, the devil, knows that we will be unable to grow spiritually or bear the fruit of the Spirit if we do not truly believe that we are the forgiven children of God.

Notice what Peter says about God's work. II Peter 1:4-9 – *"Whereby are given unto us exceeding great and precious promises: that by these ye might be partakers of the divine nature, having escaped the corruption that is in the world through lust. And beside this, giving all diligence, add to your faith virtue; and to virtue knowledge; And to knowledge temperance; and to temperance patience; and to patience godliness; And to godliness brotherly kindness; and to brotherly kindness charity. For if these things be in you, and abound, they make you that ye shall neither be barren nor unfruitful in the knowledge of our Lord Jesus Christ. But he that lacketh these things is blind, and cannot see afar off, and hath forgotten that he was purged from his old sins."* Peter is instructing us that it is dangerous to lose sight of the fact that we are forgiven in Jesus Christ. And, if we do forget, we will not develop spiritual disciplines, grow, or bear the fruit of the Spirit. Perhaps what Peter is describing in his book is where we find ourselves today. If that is the case, God would like us to be reminded of our right-standing before Him through the righteousness of Jesus Christ. God wants us to know His grace and peace once again. God wants us to know that we are forgiven and that we have become new creatures through the finished work of Jesus Christ.

Consider what the prophet, Micah, says in Micah 7:18-19 – *"Who is a God like unto thee, that pardoneth iniquity, and passeth by the transgression of the remnant of his heritage? he retaineth not his anger for ever, because he delighteth in mercy. He will turn again, he will have compassion upon us; he will subdue our iniquities; and thou wilt cast all their sins into the depths of the sea."* Also notice what the Psalmist says in Psalm 103:8-12 – *"The LORD is merciful and gracious, slow to anger, and plenteous in mercy. He will not always chide: neither will he keep his anger for ever. He hath not dealt with us after our sins; nor rewarded us according to our iniquities. For as the heaven is high above the earth, so great is his mercy toward them that fear him. As far as the east is from the west, so far hath he removed our transgressions from us."* Notice what Isaiah states through Divine inspiration of God in Isaiah 53:5-6 – *"But he was wounded for our transgressions, he was bruised for our iniquities: the chastisement of our peace was upon him; and with his stripes we are healed. All we like sheep have gone astray; we have turned every one to his own way; and the LORD hath laid on him the iniquity of us all."* Also, notice what the writer of Hebrews demonstrates in Hebrews 10:16-18 – *"This is the covenant that I will make with them after those days, saith the Lord, I will put my laws into their hearts, and in their minds will I write them; And their sins and iniquities will I remember no more. Now where remission of these is, there is no more offering for sin."* Look at what Paul told the Colossians in Colossians 2:13-15 – *"And you, being dead in your sins and the uncircumcision of your flesh, hath he quickened together with him, having forgiven you all trespasses; Blotting out the handwriting of ordinances that was against us, which was contrary to us, and took it out of the way, nailing it to his cross; And having spoiled principalities and powers, he made a shew of them openly, triumphing over them in it."*

Look at what Isaiah said in Isaiah 1:18 as well as Isaiah 44:22 – *"Come now, and let us reason together, saith the LORD: though your sins be as scarlet, they shall be as white as snow; though they be red like crimson, they shall be as wool." "I have blotted out, as a thick cloud, thy transgressions, and, as a cloud, thy sins: return unto me; for I have redeemed thee."* God is trying to demonstrate to us very vividly through the Scriptures that we are His children and are forgiven. He laid our sins on Jesus Christ and nailed them to the cross with Him. We must realize and meditate upon this fact that we are the children of God, we are forgiven, we are made free through the Lord Jesus Christ, and we are alive and complete in Him. Colossians 2:10 – *"And ye are complete in him, which is the head of all principality and power:"*

It would be wise for you at this point to take out a piece of paper and write down all the guilty things that still haunt you. Write down the things that you should have done but you did not. Then, write down the things you should not have done but you did. Lastly, write down every little bit of anger that you still have against God, yourself, and others. Take a red marker and write in big letters across the entire page – PAID IN FULL! This is the heart cry of Jesus and His finished work. He paid for our sins completely. Now, I would encourage you to take that paper and put it through a shredder several times and then take the pieces that remain and properly burn them. Watch the ashes float away in the air. Finally, realize what you have done is symbolic of what God in Christ has already done for you by grace forever.

———————

ANGER 76

nger

CHAPTER SEVEN:
GOD IS OUR SOURCE OF SUPREME JOY

I had the opportunity to be present with my wife, Linda, during the birth of our three children. I was so proud of my wife as I saw her go through the pain of giving birth to our children. It was a wonderful experience that Linda and I share together, and we are still able to share with one another even today. In addition to the pain that Linda experienced as each of our children came into the world, each of the three births had one more thing in common. Even after our children were delivered, they were still connected to Linda by their umbilical cords. It is amazing that children in the womb are united with their mothers by that cord, and in so being, what affects mom affects baby. In the case of nutrition, this is a blessing. In the case of crystal meth, crack, heroin, alcohol, tobacco, and other harmful substances, it is a tragedy. Though the mother and the child are truly separate individuals, you can accurately say that the baby is in the mother and the mother in the child. This is a tremendous illustration of the union that has taken place by grace between the Lord Jesus Christ and one of His children. In fact, for every verse in the Word of God in which Christ has said to be in us, there are several verses stating that we are "in Christ." You see, there is a spiritual umbilical cord that links us with our Savior. This is a cord that was not cut at the new birth, and it will never be severed.

It is a true saying that Jesus is in us, but also that we are in Him. We must realize that the amazing grace of God did not stop at our salvation with God saving us from an eternity in hell and preparing a place for us in Heaven to be with Him forever. There are numerous spiritual treasures that were brought out and bestowed on us the moment we accepted Jesus Christ as our Savior. Many of these wonderful treasures you may be familiar with, but you may have never thought of them as an anecdote to your problem with anger. Remember earlier in the book we said that Adam and Eve's deepest needs were met by God in the Garden of Eden. But, they were on their own to meet their needs after they chose to sin. Adam and Eve, in the flesh, were working hard seeking to regain the paradise. Only in Christ can our deep, spiritual needs of life be met.

My contention is that if a child of God truly grasps the reality on a deep heart level of how those needs are fully met in his or her Savior Jesus Christ, most of their struggles with fleshly anger will melt away. In the world in which we live today, which is a materialistic society, it is very easy to believe that the good life comes from what we possess. Jesus Christ put that thought to rest in Luke 12:15 – *"And he said unto them, Take heed, and beware of covetousness: for a man's life consisteth not in the abundance of the things which he possesseth."* The truth is this: Jesus is the *"resurrection, and the life"* (John 11:25). Jesus also is the *"way, the truth, and the life"* (John 14:6). Jesus goes on to say of Himself that He came to give us *"life…more abundantly"* (John 10:10). Our life is in Jesus Christ. We do not need to try and find life, significance, dignity, and completeness in this world because life is not a thing but a person. And, that person is the Lord Jesus Christ who lives in us, and we abide in Him.

When Paul wrote to the Colossians, he made it quite clear that when our souls are set on Christ, who is our life, then we will be empowered to put to death the deeds of the flesh. Paul is trying to make this argument in a very simple, but powerful, way. He is telling us that the old you (the you without Christ) is dead, and the new you is alive in Christ. In fact, Christ is your life and the source of your life. In Christ you already have all you need. We must realize this: What we have gained in Christ cannot be taken away from us. So, when you discover your life

(Jesus Christ), you will experience increasing victory in your struggle with anger. Why? It is because fleshly-controlled anger stems from living our lives independently of God. Knowing who we are in our Savior Jesus Christ is the Biblical path to liberation from the control of the flesh. Paul wrote in Galatians 2:20 – *"I am crucified with Christ: nevertheless I live; yet not I, but Christ liveth in me: and the life which I now live in the flesh I live by the faith of the Son of God, who loved me, and gave himself for me."* You see, by the grace of God the old fleshly you is dead and the new you is alive in Christ Jesus. Paul went on to write in Romans 6:2 – *"God forbid. How shall we, that are dead to sin, live any longer therein?"* Paul tells us in Romans 6:4-7 that we have power through the indwelling Holy Spirit of God to have victory over sin. *"Therefore we are buried with him by baptism into death: that like as Christ was raised up from the dead by the glory of the Father, even so we also should walk in newness of life. For if we have been planted together in the likeness of his death, we shall be also in the likeness of his resurrection: Knowing this, that our old man is crucified with him, that the body of sin might be destroyed, that henceforth we should not serve sin. For he that is dead is freed from sin."* As children of God, we must find ourselves consistently rejoicing that we are alive in Christ Jesus and that our spirits are eternally in union with Him.

Your struggle of who you are and what you are doing here is also over because *"as many as received him, to them gave he power to become the sons of God, even to them that believe on his name:"* (John 1:12). Many struggle in regards to their identity; they struggle with who they are. But, this need for identity is fully met in the Lord Jesus Christ as we have discussed earlier.

Another need that people have is the need for dignity. As you look back on your own life, how many times did you experience defensive anger because someone said or did something that attacked your dignity as a person? One of my patients shared with me what had been going on in her home for nearly fifteen years. Her husband was in the process of divorcing her. Over the fifteen years that they had been together, he had verbally and mentally abused her. If she voiced her opinion and it was contrary to his, she would be met by weeks of silence or outbursts of verbal abuse. Any effort she would make to exercise her authority over the children would be undermined. In every way possible he tried to make his wife look bad. She went on to say that not only was there verbal and mental abuse, but at some times there was physical abuse behind those placid suburban walls. She went on to tell me that her husband had spread false rumors about her having an affair in order to justify his separation and divorce from her. This abused and neglected woman was angry and was struggling to overcome her bitterness. This woman came to my office with headaches, but the real reason for her visit was the above. You see, this woman must realize that her hope does not lie in her husband. Her hope does not rely on her husband getting everything right between her and God.

She has no right or ability to control her husband, but these things are not determining who she is nor are they necessary for her to be alive and free in Jesus Christ. No one can keep her from being the wife and mother God created her to be. This is because her primary identity is not found in her relationship with her husband or with any other human being. Only through a relationship with God can this bewildered woman find restoration. Regardless of how her husband treated her and regardless of how her husband thought of her, she is deeply loved by God, and so are we.

David, in Psalm 27, addressed, perhaps, the most painful of all possibilities when he said, *"When my father and my mother forsake me, then the LORD will take me up"* (Psalm 27:10). This same David, as we observed earlier, knew intense rejection from King Saul. Saul tried many times to kill David. In this process, David was able write and, more importantly, live out the truth, *"Yea, though I walk through the valley of the shadow of death, I will fear no evil: for thou art with me; thy rod and thy staff they comfort me"* (Psalm 23:4). Even though family and friends may turn against us and reject us, we must realize this fact that God will never leave us nor forsake us. David knew this type of pain. He felt it deeply in his soul as his wife, Micah, mocked his exuberant worship of God as well as when his son, Absalom, attempted to overthrow his kingship.

Regardless of what others think of you, regardless of what others say of you, please listen to what God says is true about you. I Peter 2:9-10 – *"But ye are a chosen generation, a royal priesthood, an holy nation, a peculiar people; that ye should shew forth the praises of him who hath called you out of darkness into his marvellous light: Which in time past were not a people, but are now the people of God: which had not obtained mercy, but now have obtained mercy."* It is absolutely impossible for others to take those realities away from you no matter what they say and no matter what they do. You see, God knows who we really are. God is able to look upon the heart while all others are only able to look at the outside appearance. Realizing that you are unconditionally loved and accepted by God is what makes it possible to overcome your anger and walk by the Spirit when the world lets you down.

Now that we have received life through our Savior Jesus Christ and now that we realize our identity through Him and our dignity is found in Him, we are able to enjoy intimacy with God. Intimacy with God is immensely satisfying to our souls. The Psalmist knew the value of this intimate walk with God. He wrote in Psalm 73:23-28 the following: *"Nevertheless I am continually with thee: thou hast holden me by my right hand. Thou shalt guide me with thy counsel, and afterward receive me to glory. Whom have I in heaven but thee? and there is none upon earth that I desire beside thee. My flesh and my heart faileth: but God is the strength of my heart, and my portion for ever. For, lo, they that are far from thee shall perish: thou hast destroyed all them that go a whoring from thee. But it is good for me to draw near to God: I have put my trust in the Lord GOD, that I may declare all thy works."* David also wrote in Psalm 16:11 – *"Thou wilt shew me the path of life: in thy presence is fulness of joy; at thy right hand there are pleasures for evermore."*

If your relationship with God is the source of supreme joy in your life, there is far less reason to be angry.

David was a man after God's own heart, and he wrote in Psalm 27:4 – *"One thing have I desired of the LORD, that will I seek after; that I may dwell in the house of the LORD all the days of my life, to behold the beauty of the LORD, and to enquire in his temple."*

When you make the passionate pursuit of God the primary driving source in your life, you will not be disappointed. I Peter 2:6 – *"Wherefore also it is contained in the scripture, Behold, I lay in Sion a chief corner stone, elect, precious: and he that believeth on him shall not be confounded."*

With God, security and acceptance go hand in hand. Once you know you are accepted by Him, you can rest assure that He will take care of you, which brings forth a deep sense of security. When I talk about being accepted, I mean that you are received and welcomed as you are with no strings attached. This is an act of agape love or unconditional love and grace by which God the Father treats us (who were His former enemies) as His children. Notice what Jesus said in John 15:15 – *"Henceforth I call you not servants; for the servant knoweth not what his lord doeth: but I have called you friends; for all things that I have heard of my Father I have made known unto you."* This relationship of friendship carries with it the responsibility of obedience. John 15:14 – *"Ye are my friends, if ye do whatsoever I command you."*

Approximately fifteen years after the death of King Saul and his son Jonathan, King David inquired as to whether there was any surviving relative of that family to whom he could show kindness. II Samuel 9:1 – *"And David said, Is there yet any that is left of the house of Saul, that I may shew him kindness for Jonathan's sake?"* In fact, there was a surviving relative. It was the son of Jonathan whose name was Mephibosheth. Mephibosheth was living in Lo-debar and was brought before King David. When he was brought before King David, he came trembling in fear.

In those days an individual like Mephibosheth would have been put to death, but David demonstrated the grace of God.

II Samuel 9:7 – *"And David said unto him, Fear not: for I will surely shew thee kindness for Jonathan thy father's sake, and will restore thee all the land of Saul thy father; and thou shalt eat bread at my table continually."* Mephibosheth had every natural reason to fear King David. David could have looked at Mephibosheth as a threat to his throne and had him put to death, but he did not. Unknown to Mephibosheth, Jonathan and David had made a covenant years earlier that each would care for the other's family. I Samuel 18:1-4 – *"And it came to pass, when he had made an end of speaking unto Saul, that the soul of Jonathan was knit with the soul of David, and Jonathan loved him as his own soul. And Saul took him that day, and would let him go no more home to his father's house. Then Jonathan and David made a covenant, because he loved him as his own soul. And Jonathan stripped himself of the robe that was upon him, and gave it to David, and his garments, even to his sword, and to his bow, and to his girdle."*

Mephibosheth was merely a beneficiary of David's grace in the name of Jonathan, his father. Mephibosheth could not believe how King David was treating him. King David was treating him with such kindness. Mephibosheth saw himself as dead and unworthy of such treatment. II Samuel 9:8 – *"And he bowed himself, and said, What is thy servant, that thou shouldest look upon such a dead dog as I am?"* What King David had given Mephibosheth was the highest honor. In being invited to eat at the king's table, Mephibosheth was then being regarded as one of the king's sons. In like manner, too many Christians today are like Mephibosheth. They tremble before a God who unconditionally loves them, and they are afraid that God has a hammer that will ultimately fall on them if they make one little mistake. Thanks be to the Lord Jesus Christ, the hammer of God has already fallen, but it has fallen on His Son and our Savior Jesus Christ! He has already died once for all our sins. Romans 6:10 – *"For in that he died, he died unto sin once: but in that he liveth, he liveth unto God."*

What we need to do as God's children is receive His unconditional love and acceptance and receive it with joy. We must understand that the position that Mephibosheth had of blessing and honor before King David was not based on any work that he had done, but it was based on grace. Mephibosheth was crippled. He needed help getting to the king's table. So, it is with us. By God's gracious acceptance of us in Christ, we are saved. By that same grace alone, we stand. Romans 5:2 – *"By whom also we have access by faith into this grace wherein we stand, and rejoice in hope of the glory of God."*

We must constantly remind ourselves that God accepts us completely and unconditionally in Christ, baggage included. God loves us because He is love. It is His nature to love us. Though God hates our sin, He loves us before we sin, after we sin, and even while we are sinning. You see, our personal sense of security comes from an eternal relationship with God that cannot be shaken. It is not based on our ability as the Apostle Paul tells us in Romans 8:31-32; 38-39 – *"What shall we then say to these things? If God be for us, who can be against us? He that spared not his own Son, but delivered him up for us all, how shall he not with him also freely give us all things? For I am persuaded, that neither death, nor life, nor angels, nor principalities, nor powers, nor things present, nor things to come, Nor height, nor depth, nor any other creature, shall be able to separate us from the love of God, which is in Christ Jesus our Lord."* God is faithful. God is responsible, and He cares for you and me. I Peter 5:7 – *"Casting all your care upon him; for he careth for you."* You and I are secure in Him.

What you need to do is release all of your needs and wants into the hands of your all-powerful, all-wise, all-loving Heavenly Father. Release to your Heavenly Father all of your anger. Let the Apostle Paul's words in Romans 8:15-17 bring comfort and healing to you. *"For ye have not received the spirit of bondage again to fear; but ye have received the Spirit of adoption, whereby we cry, Abba, Father. The Spirit itself beareth witness with our spirit, that we are the children of God: And if children, then heirs; heirs of God, and joint-heirs with Christ; if so be that we suffer with him, that we may be also glorified together."*

Many of us today are operating with a low-grade temperature of frustration because we feel that what we do in life is meaningless. If this is truly what we believe and what we meditate upon, this will lead to frustration; and ultimately, it will lead to anger. You see, this is an unnecessary burden to bear because in our Savior Jesus Christ, our lives have tremendous significance. We, as children of God, are the salt of the earth and light of the world. Matthew 5:13-14 – *"Ye are the salt of the earth: but if the salt have lost his savour, wherewith shall it be salted? it is thenceforth good for nothing, but to be cast out, and to be trodden under foot of men. Ye are the light of the world. A city that is set on an hill cannot be hid."* Whatever you might do for your life, you can still let your light shine before men as is demonstrated in Matthew 5:16 – *"Let your light so shine before men, that they may see your good works, and glorify your Father which is in heaven."*

We must come to the realization that to live our lives in a way that points people to the true God and His Son, Jesus Christ, is supremely significant whether we do it as a machinist, housewife, minister, or any other occupation. No matter what we do everyday, we must allow God to inject into our day a new sense of the eternal. True significance is related to time. What is forgotten in time is of little significance, but what is remembered for all eternity is of great significance. That is why there are no insignificant children of God. Significance in our lives comes from faithfully living in the will of God and by letting our light so shine among men.

Are you angry because you feel like you are living an insignificant life? All God is asking from you is that you become the person He has designed for you to be, and that you fulfill the ministry He has given to you in this life. II Corinthians 5:18-21 – *"And all things are of God, who hath reconciled us to himself by Jesus Christ, and hath given to us the ministry of reconciliation; To wit, that God was in Christ, reconciling the world unto himself, not imputing their trespasses unto them; and hath committed unto us the word of reconciliation. Now then we are ambassadors for Christ, as though God did beseech you by us: we pray you in Christ's stead, be ye reconciled to God. For he hath made him to be sin for us, who knew no sin; that we might be made the righteousness of God in him."*

My friends, our time on earth is short. There are countless millions that need to hear of the finished work of the Lord Jesus Christ. Regardless of your occupation, invest your life in the proclamation of the Gospel to those God has put around you. Faithfully fulfill your ministry of reconciliation and find significance in Jesus Christ.

---

nger

CHAPTER EIGHT:
BROKEN BUT FORGIVEN

Many have what the Bible calls "infirmities" or "weaknesses." Strong's concordance defines them as "feebleness (of body or mind); by [implication] malady; [moreover] frailty: disease, infirmity, sickness, weakness."** [James Strong, Strong's Exhaustive Concordance of the Bible; Nashville, TN; Abingdon, 1980]*

Infirmities or weaknesses are wounds. These can be visible or hidden. These wounds inhibit our ability to perform at a higher level. They cause us to be feeble, frail, helpless, inefficient, and deficient in strength, dignity, or power. They can be physical conditions as well as mental, emotional, and spiritual. We all have them. We all have infirmities or weaknesses in our souls that are there because of someone else's abuse, neglect, ignorance, irresponsibility, maliciousness, or foolishness. Some infirmities that we bear are the byproduct of living in a fallen, wicked world. We have all been victims of people or circumstances to one degree or another. There are no Bible promises that we will never be victimized again. As children of God, we need no longer to live as victims. That's the beauty and power of the presence of Jesus Christ as Savior in our lives.

We cannot obviously turn the clock back and change our past, but we can be free from its demoralizing power over us. When we make the simple decision to forgive others from our hearts, we set ourselves free from the past to be victorious overcomers and more than conquerors through Him. Romans 8:37 – *"Nay, in all these things we are more than conquerors through him that loved us."* I know that the pain from our past is real, and the wounds can be very raw, but we must choose to forgive. It helps us to forgive others for the wounds that they caused us. Jesus also was wounded, and He forgave. Because Jesus was wounded in like manner as we are, He does not view our infirmities coldly or dispassionately. On the other hand, He views them very intimately and passionately for He understands. Hebrews 4:15-16 – *"For we have not an high priest which cannot be touched with the feeling of our infirmities; but was in all points tempted like as we are, yet without sin."* Our Savior, the Lord Jesus Christ, went through the worst suffering any individual has ever gone through. He went through tremendous rejection, torture, and abuse. We cannot comprehend the horror of the Holy One becoming sin for us. II Corinthians 5:21 – *"For he hath made him to be sin for us, who knew no sin; that we might be made the righteousness of God in him."* Yet, throughout all the hell He went through, Jesus NEVER sinned! In realizing all the suffering that Jesus endured, we must realize that our suffering is not a license to sin. Infirmity is not an excuse for iniquity. When we experience hurts or we are wounded, it does not give us permission to get bitter or angry. Being wounded does not give us permission to wound others. When we are wounded, we cry out, "This isn't fair!" It seems right that we only pay back the individuals for what they did to us.

We must remember Peter's description of how Jesus Christ handled the excruciating pain that sinful men inflicted upon Him and note the ramifications for those of us who are His followers. I Peter 2:19-23 – *"For this is thankworthy, if a man for conscience toward God endure grief, suffering wrongfully. For what glory is it, if, when ye be buffeted for your faults, ye shall take it patiently? but if, when ye do well, and suffer for it, ye take it patiently, this is acceptable with God. For even hereunto were ye called: because Christ also suffered for us, leaving us an example, that ye should follow his steps: Who did no sin, neither was guile found in his mouth: Who, when he was reviled, reviled not again; when he suffered, he threatened not; but committed himself to him that judgeth righteously:"* Obviously, we are not going to treat our fellow man in the same sinless treatment that Jesus Christ gave them. Though God has extended to us total forgiveness in Christ, we have not always extended that same mercy and grace toward those who have hurt us. Most often, we harbor bitterness and anger along with resentment toward others.

We must realize that forgiveness is the only way out. When Peter asked Jesus how many times it was necessary to forgive, the disciple volunteered what must have seemed to him a generous number – seven. Jesus, of course, told him his number was not sufficient. Jesus went on to proclaim that seventy times seven is more like it. I believe Jesus is trying to tell us that we are not to keep track, but as many times as someone sins against us, forgive them. Matthew 18:21-22 – *"Then came Peter to him, and said, Lord, how oft shall my brother sin against me, and I forgive him? till seven times? Jesus saith unto him, I say not unto thee, Until seven times: but, Until seventy times seven."*

Jesus went on to follow this statement by giving a story in Matthew 18:23-35. What happened in this story was a certain king decided to have all of his debts paid. The clock had literally run out on those who still owed him money. A man came before the king who owed the king a significant amount of money. He attempted to gather all the money he could, but he still fell short. The king decided to cut his losses by selling the man, his wife, and his children as slaves. He would put the man's home and all of his possessions on the auction block and try to get as much money for them as possible. The king had a right to do all of this because he was the king. Realizing that he was about to loose everything he owned as well as losing his family, the man fell down before the king and pleaded for mercy. Amazingly, in this story, the king heard the man's plea and cancelled the entire debt. This is an incredible story that Jesus tells us. The man was free of his debt! Everything that he was about to lose was restored. A life of slavery was exchanged for a life of freedom.

As this man left the presence of the king, the debtor then came across a man that owed him some money. In light of what just happened, it is unbelievable that the first debtor was unwilling to show mercy and cancel the debt of the second man. He actually had the man thrown into prison. Word got out and traveled back to the king who was not pleased at all. Let's go to Jesus' words to catch the ending. Matthew 18:32-34 – *"Then his lord, after that he had called him, said unto him, O thou wicked servant, I forgave thee all that debt, because thou desiredst me: Shouldest not thou also have had compassion on thy fellowservant, even as I had pity on thee? And his lord was wroth, and delivered him to the tormentors, till he should pay all that was due unto him."* What a sobering end! Jesus, however, did not stop there. He went on to add more for the sake of the disciples and you and me today. Matthew 18:35 – *"So likewise shall my heavenly Father do also unto you, if ye from your hearts forgive not every one his brother their trespasses."*

What Jesus was trying to get across was the turmoil of unforgiveness. Have you ever asked yourself the question: What was Jesus referring to when He spoke of being "handed over to the tormentors?" Jesus doesn't go on to explain what this actually means, but the root word means, "to experience pain, toil, or torment and to toss or vex." Clearly, then, the phrase the tormentors is referring to those natural or supernatural forces that cause intense pain and turmoil of the body and soul.

There is only one way out of the bondage of bitterness and anger and that is by forgiving others from the heart. Is unforgiveness an option? Are some things so terrible they should never be forgiven? Some people having had tremendous wrong done unto them may say, "How can you tell me to forgive? You don't know how much this person has hurt me." You are absolutely right. We don't understand the deep wounds that have been inflicted upon you by another. However, we do know that the person is still hurting you because the pain is still obviously there, and you are still bound to the past. You must understand that you do not heal in order to forgive. You forgive in order to heal.

I wish I had the time and the opportunity to sit down with you and hear your story and share your pain, but that is just impossible. You must realize that Jesus truly knows and understands your pain, and He is willing to hear your story, heal your wounds, and set you free from your past through forgiveness. He does so by first forgiving you of your sin and then you forgiving others of theirs. The way of healing is truly through forgiveness. Forgiveness is indeed necessary for healing. Forgiveness docs not mean tolerating sin and placing one's self back under the power of an abuser. God has never and will never tolerate sin and neither should you. You must also take appropriate steps to protect yourself from continued abuse in the future. In some cases, this may mean separation from a certain individual or individuals. It may even mean calling the police in certain situations. In some other more minor cases it may be simply learning how to say NO to people who attempt to take advantage of you and your talents. We must learn to set boundaries in our lives in order to protect us from being used by others. If you find yourself or you have a loved one in an abusive, harmful situation, please get help!

Just because we are Christians does not mean we have to passively sit by and take the injustices in life. God has ordained the authority of government to help protect us from harmful behavior and criminal activity. The local New Testament church should be willing to step in and help the hurting people God sends their way. Luke 10:29-37 – *"But he, willing to justify himself, said unto Jesus, And who is my neighbour? And Jesus answering said, A certain man went down from Jerusalem to Jericho, and fell among thieves, which stripped him of his raiment, and wounded him, and departed, leaving him half dead. And by chance there came down a certain priest that way: and when he saw him, he passed by on the other side. And likewise a Levite, when he was at the place, came and looked on him, and passed by on the other side. But a certain Samaritan, as he journeyed, came where he was: and when he saw him, he had compassion on him, And went to him, and bound up his wounds, pouring in oil and wine, and set him on his own beast, and brought him to an inn, and took care of him. And on the morrow when he departed, he took out two pence, and gave them to the host, and said unto him, Take care of him; and whatsoever thou spendest more, when I come again, I will repay thee. Which now of these three, thinkest thou, was neighbour unto him that fell among the thieves? And he said, He that shewed mercy on him. Then said Jesus unto him, Go, and do thou likewise."*

Regardless of the offense that has been done to us in the past, we are commanded in the Scriptures to forgive. Colossians 3:5-8; 12-13 – *"Mortify therefore your members which are upon the earth; fornication, uncleanness, inordinate affection, evil concupiscence, and covetousness, which is idolatry: For which things' sake the wrath of God cometh on the children of disobedience: In the which ye also walked some time, when ye lived in them. But now ye also put off all these; anger, wrath, malice, blasphemy, filthy communication out of your mouth. Put on therefore, as the elect of God, holy and beloved, bowels of mercies, kindness, humbleness of mind, meekness, longsuffering; Forbearing one another, and forgiving one another, if any man have a quarrel against any: even as Christ forgave you, so also do ye."*

We do not forgive a person for their sake. We forgive a person for our own sake. Unforgiveness holds us captive. To forgive frees us from that bondage. What is to be gained by forgiving is freedom from our past. If we fail to forgive, we can, then, experience tremendous mental torment. Even in the face of horrible atrocity, forgiveness is needed. Forgiveness is necessary if one is ever to be free from the past.

All of us have been hurt by someone else. Nursing small grudges can keep us in bondage and disrupt our fellowship with God as much as bitterness and anger. It might be that we avoid others at church, and maybe we do so because of an unkind or thoughtless word spoken many years ago. We dread family reunions because "that person" will be there, and we will be confronted by them. We might spend extra hours at work to avoid conflict at home. It all boils down to this: Unresolved anger can cause many to be defiled. Hebrews 12:15 – *"Looking diligently lest any man fail of the grace of God; lest any root of bitterness springing up trouble you, and thereby many be defiled;"*

The good news about all of this is Jesus Christ knows what it is to be wounded. He knows what it is to have suffered much more than we will ever be wounded or suffer. Jesus knows what it means to forgive for He did so on the cross. Though Jesus was fully God, He was also fully man. He suffered and died as a man; He forgave as a man. He did not secretly turn off His humanity on the cross and become dulled to the intense suffering of crucifixion. When the nails were hammered through His hands, He felt the pain. When He gasped for air, He felt real agony. When He bled, He felt real weakness. When He died, His brain and heart stopped; working. When He said, *"Father, forgive them; for they know not what they do"* (Luke 23:34), He gave real hope. For the same Jesus lives in all true children of God, and He is always there to give us the grace to forgive.

For some people the hardest individual to forgive is themselves. They look at themselves and a life that has been ravaged by their own choices. Their hearts are racked with guilt, shame, and regret. One of the men in the Reformers Unanimous School of Discipleship home that I dealt with in my medical office gave me the following testimony: "I am still learning from day to day to be free from my anger. God has allowed me to come a long way, but I know I still have a long way to go. As a child, I grew up in a very violent home. I was sexually abused by multiple family members. My parents ultimately got divorced, and I dealt with all the negative ramifications that come with any divorce. My family was middle-class, and my mom and dad were always concerned about looking good and proper to others, especially those inside the church. I found myself having angry outbursts toward everyone and everything. I was consumed with unforgiveness. My unforgiveness led me to many destructive behaviors including drugs and pornography. When I accepted Jesus Christ as my Savior, many things in my life were healed, and I experienced, for the first time in my life, true freedom. My anger was not so easily conquered. I have spent the last six months at Reformers Unanimous learning who I am in Jesus Christ and how to forgive others and also, and maybe more importantly, how to forgive myself. I thank God for His grace, mercy, and love, and for the freedom I am experiencing through His power."

Though we are convinced of the power of the shed blood of Jesus Christ cleansing others from their sins, sometimes we view ourselves as the exception. Seeing first hand how we messed up our lives and the lives of others, we listen to the accuser of the brethren as he relentlessly assaults us with his pack of lies. Because we instinctively know sin should be punished, we allow his brutal barrage to continue, feeling it is justified. We have come to believe that we should feel bad for what we've done.

Is this your life I am describing? Then it is time to stop giving in to the accuser. It is time to stop listening to and believing his lies; lies such as: My life is ruined and beyond repair. God does not want me. God will not forgive me. But, God does want you, and He will forgive you. God will give you the strength to forgive yourself.

There is another area of forgiveness we must deal with before we close this chapter and that concerns our dealing with anger towards God. The best book that I have found on this subject is found in the Bible, and that book is the book of Job. Though this subject is vast and far beyond the scope of this book, I do want to address this sensitive subject briefly. One of the best pieces of advice I can give you in dealing with being angry with God is to be real with God. In fact, you simply cannot be right with God until you are real with Him. And, really, the principle applies whether your anger is directed at God, other people, or even yourself. God already knows your pain and anger. Therefore, you will neither hurt nor surprise Him by being honest. God can take it. You can't take not being honest. Suppressing your emotions or holding onto your anger can damage and possibly destroy you.

The Prophet Jeremiah was in despair and depression as he

helplessly watched the destruction of his country. He was clearly depressed, but he was also very angry with God. He wrote about it in the book of Lamentations. Lamentations 3:1-3; 5-8; 10-11; 14-15; 17-18 – *"I am the man that hath seen affliction by the rod of his wrath. He hath led me, and brought me into darkness, but not into light. Surely against me is he turned; he turneth his hand against me all the day. He hath builded against me, and compassed me with gall and travail. He hath set me in dark places, as they that be dead of old. He hath hedged me about, that I cannot get out: he hath made my chain heavy. Also when I cry and shout, he shutteth out my prayer. He was unto me as a bear lying in wait, and as a lion in secret places. He hath turned aside my ways, and I was a derision to all my people; and their song all the day. He hath filled me with bitterness, he hath made me drunken with wormwood. And thou hast removed my soul far off from peace: I forgat prosperity. And I said, My strength and my hope is perished from the LORD:"* Were Jeremiah's words true? I guess in one sense they were. They were a true representation of how he felt inside. But, were they true in their depiction of God? Is God really like a bear or lion to His people? No, not at all.

Jeremiah could not have reached back into his heart and recovered the truth about who God really is without first telling the truth about how he really felt. Listen to the change of the prophet's perception of God once he was able to be emotionally honest. Lamentations 3:19-25 – *"Remembering mine affliction and my misery, the wormwood and the gall. My soul hath them still in remembrance, and is humbled in me. This I recall to my mind, therefore have I hope. It is of the LORD's mercies that we are not consumed, because his compassions fail not. They are new every morning: great is thy faithfulness. The LORD is my portion, saith my soul; therefore will I hope in him. The LORD is good unto them that wait for him, to the soul that seeketh him."*

Perhaps you are angry with God today because He did not stop the abuse you went through as a child or even as an adult. You cried out to Him, and it seemed as though He turned a deaf ear to your cries. You felt crushed and perhaps concluded that you were on your own in this world. Maybe you refused to take the risk of leaning on anyone else because you were convinced that no one, not even God, could be trusted. Perhaps you have seen the devastating suffering of a loved one and God seemed to be very distant and uncaring.

Whatever situation fits you, I would like to tell you that there is freedom for you if you are willing to face some difficult issues. There are some fundamental steps that you must take. These steps are necessary to bring about recovery and healing. These eleven steps will require your cooperation as you step out in faith.

1. You must be real with God.
2. You must be emotionally honest with your Savior.
3. You must not hide or try to minimize your anger.
4. You must admit to God and yourself that you do not have all the answers.
5. You must admit to yourself that you do not possess all wisdom and understanding.
6. You must, by faith, tell God you believe that His ways and thoughts are higher than yours. (Isaiah 55:8-9)
7. You must release the right to have all your questions answered this side of Heaven.
8. You must make the choice to release your anger toward God. (Proverbs 19:3)
9. You must prayerfully ask the Lord to reveal Himself to you in your painful memories; not angrily demanding Him to do this but humbly asking Him to touch you and heal your hurt.

---

nger
CHAPTER NINE: FORGIVENESS

We need to make sure we understand what forgiveness is and what it isn't. **Mark 11:25 –** *"And when ye stand praying, forgive, if ye have ought against any: that your Father also which is in heaven may forgive you your trespasses."* Biblically, then, someone owes a debt when another person is holding something against him or her. To forgive means that the one offended cancels the debt and releases the offender from any obligation to pay back or make restitution. It is always good when the offender asks for forgiveness and makes all and any restitution possible. But, when we forgive, we cease to demand that either be done. When someone sins against you, it is like throwing a heavy chain around your neck or casting a strong fishing line toward you and snagging you with the hook. You feel the crushing burden and pain of what was done to you. The longer you hang onto your anger, the heavier the burden becomes and more deeply the hook sets in.

The results of not forgiving are devastating. The pain that you initially felt from the offense is only compounded by your choice to not forgive. When you try to get back at the offender by remaining angry at them, you are actually bringing torment to your own soul. You have already suffered from the acts of abuse or neglect from the individual. You are now suffering from bitterness and anger. For some unknown reason, what is detrimental to our own spiritual health is that we think.

We often believe that by staying bitter we will get back at the one who has hurt us. Unfortunately, it only hurts us. This is why we are warned to not take revenge in Romans 12:17-21 – *"Recompense to no man evil for evil. Provide things honest in the sight of all men. If it be possible, as much as lieth in you, live peaceably with all men. Dearly beloved, avenge not yourselves, but rather give place unto wrath: for it is written, Vengeance is mine; I will repay, saith the Lord. Therefore if thine enemy hunger, feed him; if he thirst, give him drink: for in so doing thou shalt heap coals of fire on his head. Be not overcome of evil, but overcome evil with good."*

You must forgive to be free from your past. When you forgive, you are actually throwing the chain off your neck and pulling the hook out of your flesh. You are free though you may still be wounded emotionally. Healing will still need to take place. The good news is that now it can take place because the wounding agent has been removed through forgiveness. How long does it take your emotions to heal? It depends on how badly you were crushed and wounded by the offense and how long you have harbored unforgiveness. God does promise to nurse us back to health, for Jesus has come to *"bind up the brokenhearted, to proclaim liberty to the captives, and the opening of the prison to them that are bound"* (Isaiah 61:1). In Psalm 34:18 the Bible teaches us, *"The LORD is nigh unto them that are of a broken heart; and saveth such as be of a contrite spirit."*

You may ask yourself this question: What about the offender? Why should I let him off the hook? This is precisely why you should forgive. You will no longer be hooked to him or her. We must remember the fact that the people that we ultimately forgive are off our hooks but they are not off God's hook until they come to Christ for their own salvation, forgiveness, and cleansing. Unfortunately, some of these individuals will never come to know Jesus Christ as their personal Savior. If they do not come to know Jesus Christ as their personal Savior, these perpetrators of evil will discover that Jesus Christ, the gracious Savior, will become to them Jesus Christ, the righteous Judge. They will learn that *"It is a fearful thing to fall into the hands of the living God"* (Hebrews 10:31).

Forgiveness can be an extremely painful process, but it is the only way to stop the pain. If we do not forgive the perpetrator, we will often set out seeking revenge. If revenge is not possible, we will start to rationalize our attitudes and actions and seek other options at getting back at the other person.

God may give you, through the leadership of His Holy Spirit, a compassion for the individual who wronged you. You must realize that the one who abused you might have been abused as a child. This may genuinely help you to forgive, but having such understanding is not a substitute for forgiveness. What the individual did or said against you was wrong no matter what the reason or excuse. You still need to make a choice to forgive regardless of the other individual's attitude afterwards. Time may help heal all wounds, but it will not remove the crushing chain or the piercing hook of the offense. These are only removed when we forgive.

I do find in the Bible that it is appropriate to ask for God's mercy on the offender. Jesus said, *"Love your enemies, bless them that curse you, do good to them that hate you, and pray for them which despitefully use you, and persecute you"* (Matthew 5:44). It is also in the Bible to confess your sin of bitterness, anger, and unforgiveness. He taught us how to pray in Matthew 6:12 – *"And forgive us our debts, as we forgive our debtors."* Jesus goes on to emphasize the point that it is necessary to forgive. He emphasizes this point by letting us know that if we do not forgive others for their transgressions against us, our Heavenly Father will not forgive us of our transgressions against Him. Matthew 6:14-15 – *"For if ye forgive men their trespasses, your heavenly Father will also forgive you: But if ye forgive not men their trespasses, neither will your Father forgive your trespasses."*

When you run into a significant blockage in coronary artery disease, you can simply bypass it. However, there are no bypasses around the responsibility we have to forgive from the heart. Jesus is not teaching in Matthew, chapter six, that a true born-again believer will go to hell if he or she does not forgive another person. If you are a true born-again believer, your destiny is not at stake but your daily victory is. Though you remain His child, you will not experience the blessings and benefits of that relationship on earth. You will, however, experience torment. The restoration of the blessing of daily victory comes only when you choose to forgive.

Forgiveness does not mean that we forget the sin. Forgetting may be a long-term by-product of forgiving, but it is never a means of forgiving. What the Bible teaches us in Hebrews 10:17 (*"And their sins and iniquities will I remember no more."*) is not leading us to think that God forgets. God could not forget even if He wanted to since He is omniscient or all-knowing. It means that He will not bring up our past sins and use them against us. When we keep bringing up other individual's past offenses, we are actually saying, "I have not forgiven you."

Like most other traumatic experiences we have dealt with in our lives, our memories of sins committed against us will fade. We should not feel guilty if we remember them. However, we should not meditate on them, or our emotions will be stirred up again. When we forgive, we will find that the sting is gone even if the memories are not. Our memories will not be filled with the pain and torment we once experienced before exercising the grace and mercy of forgiveness. There is a group of individuals out there who teach and proclaim that forgiveness is impossible. Whatever God has commanded us to do we can do by His grace. God cannot do our forgiving for us, but He will empower us through the power of the Holy Spirit to do that which He has commanded us.

For some of God's people who have not been terribly hurt or who have not been neglected or abused and who struggle only mildly with anger, the thought of forgiveness is no big deal. It is like taking a walk up a very small hill. For others who have been terribly hurt, neglected, and abused and who have been harboring anger for years, the thought of exercising forgiveness may be like climbing the highest mountain. It seems like an insurmountable task. Whether it be a small hill or a mighty mountain, Jesus Christ will make the climb with you every step of the way. The freedom and exhilaration at the top are well worth the climb.

When we forgive, we must forgive from the heart. Matthew 18:35 – *"So likewise shall my heavenly Father do also unto you, if ye from your hearts forgive not every one his brother their trespasses."* Forgiveness is a soulical process. It is soulical because the heart is found in the soul. Our spirit communes with His Spirit that we are to forgive others, and then our spirit instructs our soul to forgive. By the grace of God, we can forgive from the heart. Forgiveness must come from the heart, which is the core of our being. Only in the heart does the mind, emotions, and will come together. Forgiveness has to come from the core of our being. The only successful way we know to do this is to say, "Lord, I forgive this person." If you are not willing to face the hurt and the hate, your attempt will not be successful. Trust God to bring to your mind all those things you need to forgive. Trust Him to bring to your mind every offense. You see, we have to be emotionally vulnerable to be emotionally free. Christ already knows what you are thinking and feeling. When we forgive from the heart, we are forgiving as Christ has forgiven us. Christ forgave us by taking our sins upon Himself. By forgiving others, we are agreeing to live as Jesus did.

We are all living with the consequences of other people's sins. We are all living with the consequences of Adam's sin. The only choice we have is whether we will live with the consequences of other's sins in the bondage of bitterness and anger or in the freedom of forgiveness. The sinless Lamb of God paved the way for our forgiveness and has granted us the grace to forgive as we have been forgiven. Isaiah 53:4-6 – *"Surely he hath borne our griefs, and carried our sorrows: yet we did esteem him stricken, smitten of God, and afflicted. But he was wounded for our transgressions, he was bruised for our iniquities: the chastisement of our peace was upon him; and with his stripes we are healed. All we like sheep have gone astray; we have turned every one to his own way; and the LORD hath laid on him the iniquity of us all."*

The deepest wounds that we have experienced at the hands of others can become the deepest channels of God's power, grace, and love flowing in and through our lives if we make the choice to forgive and endure the temporary consequences of sin. You see, nothing good can come from holding onto our anger and bitterness. Ephesians 4:26-27 tells us, *"Be ye angry, and sin not: let not the sun go down upon your wrath: Neither give place to the devil."* Paul urges the church at Corinth to forgive. II Corinthians 2:11 – *"Lest Satan should get an advantage of us: for we are not ignorant of his devices."* The devil can take advantage of an entire church when the members are unwilling to forgive. Paul also exhorted us to *"Let all bitterness, and wrath, and anger, and clamour, and evil speaking, be put away from you, with all malice"* (Ephesians 4:31). Unforgiveness is cancer to our souls and to the life of a church.

We must be kind and compassionate to one another. We must forgive as Christ has forgiven us. Ephesians 4:32 – *"And be ye kind one to another, tenderhearted, forgiving one another, even as God for Christ's sake hath forgiven you."* Forgiveness is the only surgery that will work on such a malignancy. Jesus declared that His shed blood and sacrificial death was the total payment for the sins of mankind including the sins committed against us. We are commanded to forgive others. It is really for our sake that we forgive others.

I urge you with all we have in Christ to take time right now to forgive those who have offended you. Even if it was years ago, I urge you to let the perpetrators off your hook so Christ can be free to bring His healing power to your wounded soul.

---

nger

CHAPTER TEN:
OUR THOUGHT PROCESS

Though the earth belongs to the Lord (Psalm 24:1), and though God loves the people of the world (John 3:16), all is not well on planet earth. There is a world system that is bent on following the devil's devices and ignoring God and His Word. In I John 2:15-17, we are admonished to not be governed by this world's system. *"Love not the world, neither the things that are in the world. If any man love the world, the love of the Father is not in him. For all that is in the world, the lust of the flesh, and the lust of the eyes, and the pride of life, is not of the Father, but is of the world. And the world passeth away, and the lust thereof: but he that doeth the will of God abideth for ever."* John's conclusion is found in I John 5:19 – *"And we know that we are of God, and the whole world lieth in wickedness."* It is obvious that no matter how wonderful the earth may seem to be at any given moment, there is a system of beliefs that drives a very ugly side of life on our planet. This system is composed of fleshly lust and the pride of men and is being directed by the devil. It is, in all practical points, anti-God. John warns that it is simply impossible to love this world's system and the Father at the same time.

We must understand that the physical world that we live in is not our enemy, nor is the world itself evil. What is evil is the philosophies that are held by the people of this world that are in direct opposition to the will of God. Just like there is nothing wrong with cell phones, pagers, laptops, and the whole lineup of technological gadgets that are commonplace in our world today. Properly used, some of these technological gadgets can serve to improve the quality of life and even spread the Gospel of Jesus Christ. But, they can also become an obsession or be used in a way that could tear a person down instead of building a person up in the Lord Jesus Christ. As we live in this world, we tend to adopt certain philosophies of this world, which are anti-God. In adopting these certain philosophies that are anti-God, we begin to deal with the stresses of life in an ungodly way. Even though these patterns are non-Christian in origin, we must be honest with ourselves and admit that they possibly have crept into our thought process even though we are reluctant to admit it.

I would like to go over **three myths** that are prevalent in our thought process, even as Christians today.

FIRST: **Materialism** – One of the world's philosophies that gives birth to many of the false beliefs that we hold on to is materialism. The dictionary defines materialism as, "the tendency to be more concerned with material than with spiritual goals or values." It is the *"love of money"* that Paul warned about as the root of all evil. I Timothy 6:10 – *"For the love of money is the root of all evil: which while some coveted after, they have erred from the faith, and pierced themselves through with many sorrows."* A materialist falsely believes that the possession of things can bring the fruit of the Spirit – love, joy, peace, etc. It can't! Those are only brought about by an individual walking in the Spirit. Materialism is very commonplace in our culture. Many people want their piece of the materialistic pie given rise to a sense of "entitlement." Entitlement lives by the philosophy of "I deserve _____" simply because I am me. Because there is so much stuff available, many people believe it should be available to them and available immediately. We see this very prevalent in our younger generation. The result of such thinking is billions of dollars of credit card debt in our nation and daily tension and anger in families because of financial stress. Though we may deny that we are materialistic, it is next to impossible to live in a culture such as ours and not be affected or even infected to some extent with materialism.

Are you worshipping "dead gods?" The American dream can easily become the American nightmare. The ancient words of Psalm 135:15-18 describe the root of the problem. *"The idols of the heathen are silver and gold, the work of men's hands. They have mouths, but they speak not; eyes have they, but they see not; They have ears, but they hear not; neither is there any breath in their mouths. They that make them are like unto them: so is every one that trusteth in them."* Scripture warns that you become like the god you worship. If you worship the true and living God, you will be alive and made free by the truth. However, if your goal is cold, hard cash and the lifeless things it can buy, what kind of person do you expect you will become? The Bible has much to say about materialism. Matthew 8:20 – *"And Jesus saith unto him, The foxes have holes, and the birds of the air have nests; but the Son of man hath not where to lay his head."* It is crucial to realize that Jesus wasn't whining or complaining in the above Scripture. He was not engaging in a little messianic self-pity. He was simply telling it like it was. No palatial estates guaranteed and not even the best lawn in the subdivision. Jesus slept His first night on earth in a stable, and nothing changed much over the next thirty years for Him. He warned us. Luke 12:15 – *"And he said unto them, Take heed, and beware of covetousness: for a man's life consisteth not in the abundance of the things which he possesseth."*

SECOND: **Pleasure** – In addition to warning us about loving money, the Apostle Paul also warned us about another dangerous philosophy of life. He called it being *"lovers of pleasure"* and warned that it stands in direct conflict of being *"lovers of God"* (II Timothy 3:4). This is a philosophy that many have adapted; the pursuit of pleasure apart from God rather than the pursuit of pleasure in God. When we adopt this philosophy of pleasure apart from God and the feel-good god is not appeased, we become irritated, annoyed, and even angry. As we try to eliminate suffering from our society, we have only become angrier and more anxious when that inevitable suffering arrives. We must realize that Jesus learned obedience from the things He suffered. Hebrews 5:8 – *"Though he were a Son, yet learned he obedience by the things which he suffered;"*

If the Son of God went through such training in life, what makes us think that we can learn to walk with the Father by an easier way?

THIRD: **Selfishness** – Another worldly philosophy that fuels societal anger is selfishness manifested in a drive to compete, get ahead, and win at all cost. Whereas, materialism is the lust of the eyes in action and seeking pleasure is the lust of the flesh, selfishness is the boastful pride of life. It is not so much the obsessive desire for things as it is the proud yearning to be top dog, first, and best. It is not, "Hey, look what I've got!"; but rather, "Hey, look at me!" It is born out of men being lovers of self. II Timothy 3:2 – *"For men shall be lovers of their own selves, covetous, boasters, proud, blasphemers, disobedient to parents, unthankful, unholy,"*

My friend, selfishness can show up in Christian ministry. We must not sacrifice our families on the altars of our ministries.

Materialism, pleasure, and selfishness constitute the holy trinity of the world's system. Unless we turn to the One God, these false gods will grow bigger, stronger, and louder, demanding more and more of our attention and energy. The stakes are being raised all of the time, and the cost to our human souls is staggering. Too many of us are climbing the corporate ladder and realizing too late that it is leaning against the wrong wall.

Why not take a sober look at your life. Are you finding yourself being short with your co-workers and loved ones because you feel you are perpetually behind. When all of your energy is being drained away in an effort to keep up, you will find you have nothing left to give in your relationship. In fact, you will find that you loose your temper at the smallest intrusion of needs or demands from the people around you. With your plate too full, you end up forcing your loved ones to eat the crumbs that fall off the table.

Where is God in all of our business? We are not excusing laziness or denying the need to do our work heartily for the Lord, but why are we so stressed out so often? It is not time we lack because we have precisely the right amount of time to do God's will. The problem is that we've shoved Christ out of the center of our lives and compromised our Christian values.

If you are tired of being out of breath, out of time, and out of sorts, then the next chapter is for you. In it we will talk about how to get out of the rat race while still living in the real world.

———————————

ANGER 108

nger

CHAPTER ELEVEN: PEACE

Not surprisingly, the earthly life of Jesus Christ, the Prince of peace, provides a wonderful contrast to the hectic American way of life. Notice what He did when the pressures of life started mounting. Luke 5:15-16 – *"But so much the more went there a fame abroad of him: and great multitudes came together to hear, and to be healed by him of their infirmities. And he withdrew himself into the wilderness, and prayed."* This example of Jesus' habit is important for three reasons: First, this was a time in His earthly work when He was well known and in great demand. He was in real danger of being totally overwhelmed by the shear numbers of people coming to Him. Secondly, Jesus knew where His strength and direction came from. Though He possessed a perfect heart of compassion and love to be with people, that is not where His life came from. Rather, everything flowed to Him from the Father. Thirdly, Jesus developed a lifestyle of slipping away to pray. It had been woven into the fabric of His life on earth. It probably required a sacrifice of physical comfort. Mark 1:35 gives us insight into the "when" of Jesus' solitude. *"And in the morning, rising up a great while before day, he went out, and departed into a solitary place, and there prayed."*

In contrast to Jesus, we are a people that do not practice silence and solitude. We are a nation that has grown accustom to activity and noise, and we find it awkward to be alone and silent. Our Spiritual condition may be assessed by how we handle solitude. In the following Psalms, David admonishes us to wait in silence before God and put our trust in Him. Psalm 62:5-8 – *"My soul, wait thou only upon God; for my expectation is from him. He only is my rock and my salvation: he is my defence; I shall not be moved. In God is my salvation and my glory: the rock of my strength, and my refuge, is in God. Trust in him at all times; ye people, pour out your heart before him: God is a refuge for us. Selah."* Psalm 131 – *"LORD, my heart is not haughty, nor mine eyes lofty: neither do I exercise myself in great matters, or in things too high for me. Surely I have behaved and quieted myself, as a child that is weaned of his mother: my soul is even as a weaned child. Let Israel hope in the LORD from henceforth and for ever."* Psalm 23:1-3 – *"The LORD is my shepherd; I shall not want. He maketh me to lie down in green pastures: he leadeth me beside the still waters. He restoreth my soul: he leadeth me in the paths of righteousness for his name's sake."*

With a busy life and a full plate, I have found it crucial to get up early to meet with God before the rest of the house rises. Jesus talked about praying to the Father in secret either in a room or a closet. He promised that your Father who sees you there will reward you. Matthew 6:6 – *"But thou, when thou prayest, enter into thy closet, and when thou hast shut thy door, pray to thy Father which is in secret; and thy Father which seeth in secret shall reward thee openly."* Scheduling time alone with the Lord sets the stage for walking with Him during the rest of the day.

Why not take periodic "Jesus breaks" when you can just relax and just focus on Him. It could be in the shower, in the car, taking a walk with the dog, picking up the mail, or sitting in your comfortable chair. Moments of talking and even venting in God's presence can be life savers. Brief periods of time in silent reflection or worship can calm your spirit and diffuse your anger. Paul exhorted us in Romans 12:2 – *"And be not conformed to this world: but be ye transformed by the renewing of your mind, that ye may prove what is that good, and acceptable, and perfect, will of God."* If we are not actively allowing our minds to be renewed, we will, by default, be slowly but surely squeezed into this world's mold; a world that lives as if business was next to Godliness. Between His prayer that the Father would keep His disciples from the evil one (John 17:15 – *"I pray not that thou shouldest take them out of the world, but that thou shouldest keep them from the evil."*) and His request that the Father would sanctify them in the truth of the Word (John 17:17 – *"Sanctify them through thy truth: thy word is truth."*), Jesus declares, *"They are not of the world, even as I am not of the world"* (John 17:16).

Though we are in this world, we are not of it, neither is Jesus. The devil is the god of this world, and he will rule over our lives to the degree that we love this world. God's Word, however, will sanctify us and set us apart from its angry, corrupting influences. No matter how much the world has already infected us, Jesus can cleanse us. John 16:33 – *"These things I have spoken unto you, that in me ye might have peace. In the world ye shall have tribulation: but be of good cheer; I have overcome the world."*

For those who care to take the time, their place of sitting at the feet of Jesus will be a sanctuary, a refuge, and a safe haven from the stresses and pressures of an angry world. It will be a place of brokenness, introspection, quiet instruction, restoration, healing, serenity, and, finally, a place of peace. Don't be surprised if others do not understand your desire to sit at Jesus' feet. The way of freedom will always be opposed by those who don't understand or by those who don't want to give up what the world has to offer them. But, you can't let that stop you! I John 5:4-5 – *"They are of the world: therefore speak they of the world, and the world heareth them."*

Here are a few suggestions that I believe will help you experience a piece of Jesus' mind:

1. Schedule daily time to spend with the Lord.
2. Keep your time with God simple and uncomplicated.
3. Keep your time with God fresh.
4. Consider fasting.
5. Don't take yourself or your work too seriously.

Psalm 23 – "*The LORD is my shepherd; I shall not want. He maketh me to lie down in green pastures: he leadeth me beside the still waters. He restoreth my soul: he leadeth me in the paths of righteousness for his name's sake. Yea, though I walk through the valley of the shadow of death, I will fear no evil: for thou art with me; thy rod and thy staff they comfort me. Thou preparest a table before me in the presence of mine enemies: thou anointest my head with oil; my cup runneth over. Surely goodness and mercy shall follow me all the days of my life: and I will dwell in the house of the LORD for ever.*"

---

nger

CHAPTER TWELVE:
THE POWER OF GOD

It is encouraging to know that even the Apostle Paul had a struggle. In fact, every child of God can echo at some point in life Paul's words in Romans 7:15-19 – *"For that which I do I allow not: for what I would, that do I not; but what I hate, that do I. If then I do that which I would not, I consent unto the law that it is good. Now then it is no more I that do it, but sin that dwelleth in me. For I know that in me (that is, in my flesh,) dwelleth no good thing: for to will is present with me; but how to perform that which is good I find not. For the good that I would I do not: but the evil which I would not, that I do."* Confused, frustrated, paralyzed, and despairing are words that describe Paul in the verses above. It is a description of a man in bondage. It is a man who knows the truth but just does not seem able to make it happen in this life. Maybe this is where you find yourself as you read these words. Don't give up! The Helper, the Comforter, and the Holy Spirit are here.

Before we dive into the solution in Romans, chapter eight, we need to look further into the problem in Romans, chapter seven. The cure will be much more powerful once we understand the disease.

Notice that Paul's heart was righteous. He wanted to do what was right. Willing to do good was present in him. Paul did not need convincing that God's Word was right and needed to be obeyed. Paul wanted to follow God's Word. This is evidence that we are children of God. There are many who consider this passage of Scripture the "normal" Christian life. Consequently, they have felt doomed to battle their anger and rage all of their lives hoping for, at best, brief moments of victory. My friends, nothing can be further from the truth. Paul said in Romans 7:18 – *"For I know that in me (that is, in my flesh,) dwelleth no good thing: for to will is present with me; but how to perform that which is good I find not."* He did not say that he was no good nor did he say nothing good dwelled in him at all. What he did say was that nothing good dwelled in his flesh. In fact, he went on to identify the culprit. It was sin dwelling in his flesh that was operating contrary to God. We have a new identity, a new heart, and a new nature in Christ. The very presence of God dwells within us. However, there still remains a residual part of us that is bent toward self-reliant, self-centered living. In that place that the Bible calls "flesh," the power of sin resides, exercising its influence through our physical bodies. Sin is not us, but it dwells in us.

Do you feel a civil war inside of you? Do you sense the inner struggle to do what is right versus an evil presence pulling you in the other direction? The Spirit of truth working through your mind is being opposed by sin which seeks to operate through your flesh.

James 1:13-15 makes it clear that we are fully capable of generating sin by ourselves through our own fleshly lusts. *"Let no man say when he is tempted, I am tempted of God: for God cannot be tempted with evil, neither tempteth he any man: But every man is tempted, when he is drawn away of his own lust, and enticed. Then when lust hath conceived, it bringeth forth sin: and sin, when it is finished, bringeth forth death."* In addition, however, the world's system governed by Satan makes it appeal to our minds through those lusts. I John 2:15-17 – *"Love not the world, neither the things that are in the world. If any man love the world, the love of the Father is not in him. For all that is in the world, the lust of the flesh, and the lust of the eyes, and the pride of life, is not of the Father, but is of the world. And the world passeth away, and the lust thereof: but he that doeth the will of God abideth for ever.*" Finally, the devil's enticing voice coming from without can sound identical to the tempting voice of sin coming from within. In essence, we are being triple-teamed by the world, the flesh, and the devil. Sin is deceptive. Hebrews 3:13 – *"But exhort one another daily, while it is called To day; lest any of you be hardened through the deceitfulness of sin.*" It promises pleasure, fulfillment, and satisfaction; but it lies. It only delivers passing pleasures. Hebrews 11:25 – *"Choosing rather to suffer affliction with the people of God, than to enjoy the pleasures of sin for a season.*" Then, here comes the ugly payoff. The consequences are always greater than the benefits...ALWAYS!

So, if you choose to walk according to the flesh instead of the Spirit, you will find yourself crying out along with the Apostle Paul. Romans 7:24 – *"O wretched man that I am! who shall deliver me from the body of this death?*" Notice Paul did not say "wicked man that I am" but he said *"wretched man that I am.*" Wretched means "miserable." Bondage to sin will inevitably lead to misery in a Christian's life.

Despite how overwhelming the circumstances in life may be and how overwhelming the misery of walking in the flesh is to a Christian, no saved individual needs to continue walking in the flesh. The Apostle Paul, who was walking in the flesh, did not continue walking in the flesh. Listen to his words of victory in Romans 8:1-4 – *"There is therefore now no condemnation to them which are in Christ Jesus, who walk not after the flesh, but after the Spirit. For the law of the Spirit of life in Christ Jesus hath made me free from the law of sin and death. For what the law could not do, in that it was weak through the flesh, God sending his own Son in the likeness of sinful flesh, and for sin, condemned sin in the flesh: That the righteousness of the law might be fulfilled in us, who walk not after the flesh, but after the Spirit.*"

Child of God, you must remember this fact: No matter what you have done contrary to the will and Word of God, you are not condemned as you walk in the Lord Jesus Christ. God is for you! Romans 8:31 – *"What shall we then say to these things? If God be for us, who can be against us?*" God is on your side.

As you walk in the Lord Jesus Christ, you are on God's side. What has been condemned is your sin. Your sin was sentenced to death and executed. That's what happened at the cross of Calvary. Because of Calvary, you are made free from sin's hold over you and the spiritual death that was yours apart from Christ. Paul explained in Romans 6:7-8 that our old sin-loving self died with Christ. *"For he that is dead is freed from sin. Now if we be dead with Christ, we believe that we shall also live with him:"* The fact that you have been letting sin reign in your body and have been obeying its lust does not negate the fact that you are free from sin's control in Christ. Romans 6:12 – *"Let not sin therefore reign in your mortal body, that ye should obey it in the lusts thereof."* You are like a man pardoned by the judge and released from prison after years of hard labor; but this man keeps sneaking back into his jail cell.

What we need to do is notice how we make this freedom real in our experiences. Romans 8:4 – "That the righteousness of the law might be fulfilled in us, who walk not after the flesh, but after the Spirit." That was the key that was missing in Paul's Romans, chapter seven, experience. Did you notice that not once was the Holy Spirit mentioned in Paul's description of his struggle. The knowledge, and even the desire to do what was right, had been there, but the power was not! Tragically, most Christians are living in the same spiritual impotence. They are like the man who took his family to the car dealer to purchase his first car – a brand new minivan. After the man had signed the papers and made the down payment, the salesman handed him the keys and shook his hand to wish him well. The father, thrilled at his new acquisition, piled his wife and children into the van and proceeded to the rear so he could push it home. After miles of this exhausting effort, a friend pulled up alongside him driving his own car. The friend said, "Need some help? Are you out of gas?" "No," he replied. "The gas tank is full of gas." The friend then replied, "Why are you pushing it? The car is brand new!" "Yes," he said. "I was really excited about it at first, and this is hard work. I am getting more and more frustrated with the whole thing. I am beginning to think this car-driving business is not for me." The friend, realizing that his buddy was clueless, asked, "Did not the salesman give you a key to start the car?" "Oh yes," he replied. "I've got it right here in my pocket." His friend began to explain to him that there was power under the hood that would propel that vehicle effortlessly down the road. All his friend had to do was turn on the ignition, sit behind the wheel and give it some gas. So, his friend happily drove off into the sunset. This parable would never happen in real life, of course. At least not with cars! But, it is happening everyday in the spiritual realm as God's children desperately try (and fail) to live the Christian life by their own strength rather than by the power of the Holy Spirit.

Talking about the Holy Spirit makes some people very nervous. Jesus talked a lot about the coming of the Spirit just prior to His death. Here is a sample of Jesus' words in John 14:16-17, John 14:26, John 16:7, 12-14 – *"And I will pray the Father, and he shall give you another Comforter, that he may abide with you for ever; Even the Spirit of truth; whom the world cannot receive, because it seeth him not, neither knoweth him: but ye know him; for he dwelleth with you, and shall be in you. But the Comforter, which is the Holy Ghost, whom the Father will send in my name, he shall teach you all things, and bring all things to your remembrance, whatsoever I have said unto you. Nevertheless I tell you the truth; It is expedient for you that I go away: for if I go not away, the Comforter will not come unto you; but if I depart, I will send him unto you. I have yet many things to say unto you, but ye cannot bear them now. Howbeit when he, the Spirit of truth, is come, he will guide you into all truth: for he shall not speak of himself; but whatsoever he shall hear, that shall he speak: and he will shew you things to come. He shall glorify me: for he shall receive of mine, and shall shew it unto you."*

Have you ever thought about how wonderfully it would have been to be a disciple back in the days of Jesus' earthly ministry? You would have been able to experience His marvelous miracles, hear His powerful preaching and experience, first hand, His love and mercy as He healed so many. But, Jesus said it was better for us that He go away. Why? He had to go so that the Holy Spirit, the Comforter, would come. You see, while Jesus lived on the earth He limited himself to time – about 33-34 years in space. The best that people could experience in those days was to have God with them in the Person of Jesus Christ. Now, there are no limitations, and God, through the Holy Spirit, actually lives in all of His children. That reality ought to make us pause to think – The God of the universe, the One with all-power and wisdom and love, lives inside of every man, woman, and child who belongs to Him. In fact, our bodies are called the temple of the Holy Spirit. I Corinthians 6:19 – *"What? know ye not that your body is the temple of the Holy Ghost which is in you, which ye have of God, and ye are not your own?"*

Have you felt frustrated and powerless against the anger and rage in your life? If you are a child of God, that sense of despair and defeat is based on ignorance, unbelief, or a lie. The power of our Heavenly Father is greater than any sin, and this power is available within you through the Holy Spirit of God. Listen again to the instruction of the Apostle Paul as he was led by the Holy Spirit to pen Ephesians 3:20-21 – *"Now unto him that is able to do exceeding abundantly above all that we ask or think, according to the power that worketh in us, Unto him be glory in the church by Christ Jesus throughout all ages, world without end. Amen."* We must come to realize on a moment-by-moment basis that there is no power shortage with God. God is eager, willing, and able to do all that is in accordance with His will.

Perhaps the most amazing truth of all is that the power source, the generator, lives within you in the person of the Holy Spirit of God. How strong is the power of Christ? Paul wanted us to see that reality in Ephesians 1:18-23 – *"The eyes of your understanding being enlightened; that ye may know what is the hope of his calling, and what the riches of the glory of his inheritance in the saints, And what is the exceeding greatness of his power to us-ward who believe, according to the working of his mighty power, Which he wrought in Christ, when he raised him from the dead, and set him at his own right hand in the heavenly places, Far above all principality, and power, and might, and dominion, and every name that is named, not only in this world, but also in that which is to come: And hath put all things under his feet, and gave him to be the head over all things to the church, Which is his body, the fulness of him that filleth all in all."* The same mighty, awesome power that raised the Lord Jesus Christ from death to life and brought Him to God's right hand, far above all other authority, is the same strength working in you and me.

What is then being *"filled with the Spirit?"* It is when a child of God is experiencing the Holy Spirit's powerful presence in their life, guiding and directing them in what to think, say, and do. This state of Spiritual being (being filled with the Holy Spirit and walking in the Spirit) is not a luxury but a necessity. It is a command of God according to Ephesians 5:18-21 – *"And be not drunk with wine, wherein is excess; but be filled with the Spirit; Speaking to yourselves in psalms and hymns and spiritual songs, singing and making melody in your heart to the Lord; Giving thanks always for all things unto God and the Father in the name of our Lord Jesus Christ; Submitting yourselves one to another in the fear of God."* Just as drugs and alcohol radically alters the personality of the taker, so the filling of the Holy Spirit transforms the believer. Instead of angry, hurtful words, there is a flow of praise and worship from the heart through the lips. Instead of grumbling and complaining, there is thanksgiving. Instead of hostility and rebellion, there is humility and submission to the will of God.

There are **three primary prerequisites** for the filling of the Holy Spirit of God:

1.**Desire** – Jesus said, *"Blessed are they which do hunger and thirst after righteousness: for they shall be filled."* This is not a drowsy, half-hearted, "guess I could use some help" kind of desire. It is the same intense yearning and longing in the spiritual realm that a starving and thirsty man experiences in the physical realm. Jesus tells us about this in John 7:37-39 – *"In the last day, that great day of the feast, Jesus stood and cried, saying, If any man thirst, let him come unto me, and drink. He that believeth on me, as the scripture hath said, out of his belly shall flow rivers of living water. (But this spake he of the Spirit, which they that believe on him should receive: for the Holy Ghost was not yet given;*

because that Jesus was not yet glorified.)"

2.**Humility** – In order to bring us to the point of such hunger and thirst for Him, God often has to break our stubborn will. James 4:6 – *"But he giveth more grace. Wherefore he saith, God resisteth the proud, but giveth grace unto the humble."* We have been living our lives for the most part independently of God. We must come to the point where we humble ourselves under the mighty hand of God, according to I Peter 5:6 – *"Humble yourselves therefore under the mighty hand of God, that he may exalt you in due time,"* confess our sins and repent of living by our own strength and resources. It may take a lot to bring some children of God to the end of their resources so that they can discover God's resources. If necessary, God will orchestrate our own breaking through discipline.

We find in the Word of God that His discipline in our lives is in love because we are His children. Hebrews 12:5-7 – *"And ye have forgotten the exhortation which speaketh unto you as unto children, My son, despise not thou the chastening of the Lord, nor faint when thou art rebuked of him: For whom the Lord loveth he chasteneth, and scourgeth every son whom he receiveth. If ye endure chastening, God dealeth with you as with sons; for what son is he whom the father chasteneth not?"* His disciplines are not only in love because we are His children, but they are for our good so that we may share His holiness. Hebrews 12:10 – *"For they verily for a few days chastened us after their own pleasure; but he for our profit, that we might be partakers of his holiness."* God knows that living according to the flesh is futile. Therefore, He allows us to come to our own painful conclusion about the futility of our own self-centered ways. Hopefully, we will be wise enough to surrender to His will.

3.**Faith** – Faith is the third prerequisite for being filled with the Holy Spirit of God. Hebrews 11:6 – *"But without faith it is impossible to please him: for he that cometh to God must believe that he is, and that he is a rewarder of them that diligently seek him."* Do you believe that God will reward you when you seek Him to fill you with the Spirit? If you do, that is faith. Jesus showed us God's eagerness to fill us with the Holy Spirit. Luke 11:11-13 – *"If a son shall ask bread of any of you that is a father, will he give him a stone? or if he ask a fish, will he for a fish give him a serpent? Or if he shall ask an egg, will he offer him a scorpion? If ye then, being evil, know how to give good gifts unto your children: how much more shall your heavenly Father give the Holy Spirit to them that ask him?"* God wants you to be filled with His Holy Spirit.

What we need is for the life of Christ to be fully manifested in our bodies, souls, and spirits. This is glorifying God in our bodies, that is, to manifest the presence of God. The Spirit-filled life is essentially the same as abiding in Christ who is our life. The Lord Jesus spoke explicitly about this intimate connection in John 15:4-5 – *"Abide in me, and I in you. As the branch cannot bear fruit of itself, except it abide in the vine; no more can ye, except ye abide in me. I am the vine, ye are the branches: He that abideth in me, and I in him, the same bringeth forth much fruit: for without me ye can do nothing."*

The branch of a grapevine does not generate the fruit that hangs from it by itself. The life, energy, and nourishment that create the fruit flow up through the vine and into the branch. Apart from the vine the branch will be useless and fruitless, but a branch properly connected to the vine will bear fruit. So it is with our relationship with Jesus. If we try to live the Christian life in our own strength, we cannot bear fruit because the fruit of the Christian can only be the fruit of the Spirit. Galatians 5:22-23 – *"But the fruit of the Spirit is love, joy, peace, longsuffering, gentleness, goodness, faith, Meekness, temperance: against such there is no law."* The only power source capable of producing such fruit is the Holy Sprit who dwells within us.

An outburst of anger is a deed of the flesh according to Galatians 5:20-21 – *"Idolatry, witchcraft, hatred, variance, emulations, wrath, strife, seditions, heresies, Envyings, murders, drunkenness, revellings, and such like: of the which I tell you before, as I have also told you in time past, that they which do such things shall not inherit the kingdom of God."* The goal is not simply to stop the deeds of the flesh. The goal is to be filled with the Spirit.

- ▶ Love must replace hate.
  - ▶ Joy must replace grumbling.
  - ▶ Peace must replace anxiety.
  - ▶ Patience must replace anger.
  - ▶ Kindness must replace hostility.
  - ▶ Goodness must replace malice.
  - ▶ Faithfulness must replace a lack of trust.
  - ▶ Gentleness must replace rudeness.

Finally, we have Spirit control where before we lost control. We have a choice as to whether we are going to live by the Spirit or live according to the flesh. These two are in direct opposition of each other according to Paul in Galatians 5:16-17 – *"This I say then, Walk in the Spirit, and ye shall not fulfil the lust of the flesh. For the flesh lusteth against the Spirit, and the Spirit against the flesh: and these are contrary the one to the other: so that ye cannot do the things that ye would."*

Mark tells us that Jesus sent the disciples out across the Sea of Galilee after feeding the five thousand. Mark 6:45 – *"And straightway he constrained his disciples to get into the ship, and to go to the other side before unto Bethsaida, while he sent away the people."* The Master, however, stayed behind to pray on the mountain. Late that night Jesus and the disciples had an encounter; one that can change our lives just as it did theirs. Mark 6:48-50 – *"And he saw them toiling in rowing; for the wind was contrary unto them: and about the fourth watch of the night he cometh unto them, walking upon the sea, and would have passed by them. But when they saw him walking upon the sea, they supposed it had been a spirit, and cried out: For they all saw him, and were troubled. And immediately he talked with them, and saith unto them, Be of good cheer: it is I; be not afraid."* Many of us are like the disciples. We are struggling and straining, trying to live the Christian life in our own power. If you want to row against the storms of life, go ahead. God will let you do so until you collapse in exhaustion. Jesus always intends to pass by the self-sufficient person. As long as we think we can do it ourselves, He will let us. When the disciples acknowledged their need for help, Jesus came to them. He responded immediately once they admitted their weaknesses.

Isn't it time to break the cycle of defeat in your life? If that is your desire, ask God today to fill you with His Holy Spirit.

———————————

ANGER 124

nger

CHAPTER THIRTEEN:
HOW TO HAVE VICTORY OVER ANGER

Realize that we are now no longer in Adam, but we are now in Christ. When we receive Jesus Christ as our Savior, we become dead to sin. This means that we are no longer slaves to sin. It means that sin is no longer our master. Romans 6:14 – *"For sin shall not have dominion over you: for ye are not under the law, but under grace."* We make this statement because we realize that the power of sin has been broken through the Lord Jesus Christ. By the enabling grace of God and through the empowerment of the Holy Spirit of God, we can say NO to sin. We do not have to follow sin any longer. We, however, can choose to walk in the Spirit; and if we do so, the Bible tells us that we will not fulfill the lust of the flesh. Galatians 5:16-17 – *"This I say then, Walk in the Spirit, and ye shall not fulfil the lust of the flesh. For the flesh lusteth against the Spirit, and the Spirit against the flesh: and these are contrary the one to the other: so that ye cannot do the things that ye would."*

This truth that we have just described has tremendous ramifications for believers controlled by fleshly anger and rage. You see, all excuses are gone but so is our helplessness. We cannot say, "I just can't help it. That's the way I am." That is not true if we have Jesus Christ as our Savior. We now can say, "In Christ and through the indwelling of the Holy Spirit I can live a righteous life." Knowing all of this truly brings us hope. I have hope because now I am not alone. I am not abandoned. I am not helpless or hopeless. I have a great future in the Lord

Jesus Christ. In fact, I have a great "now" in the Lord Jesus Christ.

STEP TWO – I realize that as I walk this earth every day that I will still have a problem with anger, which is sin. I realize that by myself I am incapable of overcoming its control over me.

The truth of our new identity in the Lord Jesus Christ and that His Holy Spirit now indwells us does not negate the reality that all of us battle flesh patterns to one degree or another. It is a denial of reality when we refuse to face the fact that clearly indicates we have a problem with fleshly anger. Healing only comes when we courageously face the truth that we have a problem beyond our ability to solve. Pride will try to deceive us into thinking we can overcome our anger in our own strength. John 15:5 – *"I am the vine, ye are the branches: He that abideth in me, and I in him, the same bringeth forth much fruit: for without me ye can do nothing."*

Do you get angry easily? Do people say you have a temper? Is anger an emotion you readily display or never dare to show? Do you believe you have a right to be angry? Do you require medication to relieve stress or stress-related maladies? Are you uptight? Do you find yourself easily irritated or impatient? Do you resent other drivers in vehicles on the road? Are you a sore loser? Do you intend to get upset over matters that you have little or no ability to control? If any of these statements are true, you need to meditate on the following verses found in the book of Proverbs:

Proverbs 12:16 – *"A fool's wrath is presently known: but a prudent man covereth shame."*

Proverbs 14:29 – *"He that is slow to wrath is of great understanding: but he that is hasty of spirit exalteth folly."*

Proverbs 16:32 – *"He that is slow to anger is better than the mighty; and he that ruleth his spirit than he that taketh a city."*

Proverbs 19:11 – *"The discretion of a man deferreth his anger; and it is his glory to pass over a transgression."*

Proverbs 19:19 – *"A man of great wrath shall suffer punishment: for if thou deliver him, yet thou must do it again."*

Proverbs 22:24-25 – *"Make no friendship with an angry man; and with a furious man thou shalt not go: Lest thou learn his ways, and get a snare to thy soul."*

Proverbs 29:11 – *"A fool uttereth all his mind: but a wise man keepeth it in till afterwards."*

In the Christian walk we do not try to control or manipulate others through anger. God calls people who do this "fools," and He is not the least bit impressed by their ability to angrily manipulate people and circumstances. In fact, Scripture warns that such people will fall into trouble as will those who hang around them.

We must come to the realization that we cannot help ourselves. Getting out of denial and coming face to face with the anger problem is essential to the healing process. David once kept silent about his sin, and he shared the consequences of his cover-up in Psalm 32:3-4 – *"When I kept silence, my bones waxed old through my roaring all the day long. For day and night thy hand was heavy upon me: my moisture is turned into the drought of summer. Selah."* David's psychosomatic illness was due to unconfessed sin, which finally led him to walk in the light. Psalm 32:5 – *"I acknowledged my sin unto thee, and mine iniquity have I not hid. I said, I will confess my transgressions unto the LORD; and thou forgavest the iniquity of my sin. Selah."* The Lord won't let one of His children live in denial because He loves them too much. Jeremiah wrote, *"Also in thy skirts is found the blood of the souls of the poor innocents: I have not found it by secret search, but upon all these. Yet thou sayest, Because I am innocent, surely his anger shall turn from me. Behold, I will plead with thee, because thou sayest, I have not sinned"* (Jeremiah 2:34-35).

Do not make the mistake of ignoring or denying your anger problem. God's grace for healing awaits, but it is only to the humble man that He gives it according to James 4:6 – *"But he giveth more grace. Wherefore he saith, God resisteth the proud, but giveth grace unto the humble."* Do not resist God's humbling process as He breaks down your fleshly defenses and brings you to the end of your own resources. Psalm 51:17 – *"The sacrifices of God are a broken spirit: a broken and a contrite heart, O God, thou wilt not despise."* You may find it very painful to see your coping mechanisms crumble. You may not like what you see in yourself at all but know that the Lord will never despise you as you come face to face with your weakness and the failure of your flesh.

STEP THREE – The only hope that I have for breaking free from anger's control is through the presence and power of the Holy Spirit of God in my life.

Neither this person nor this book I have written has any power to set you free from the power of sin. The power to deliver you and me from any sin lies solely in the Lord Jesus Christ and in the indwelling Holy Spirit of God as He guides us in the truth of His Word. The Holy Spirit can and does work through a book, seminar, sermon, pastor, or counselor as His instruments, but it is the Son who makes us free. John 8:32 – *"And ye shall know the truth, and the truth shall make you free."*

If you are putting your trust in any person, including yourself or any human method, your faith will prove misguided and futile. Romans 9:33 – *"As it is written, Behold, I lay in Sion a stumblingstone and rock of offence: and whosoever believeth on him shall not be ashamed."* Jeremiah 17:5-8 – *"Thus saith the LORD; Cursed be the man that trusteth in man, and maketh flesh his arm, and whose heart departeth from the LORD. For he shall be like the heath in the desert, and shall not see when good cometh; but shall inhabit the parched places in the wilderness, in a salt land and not inhabited. Blessed is the man that trusteth in the LORD, and whose hope the LORD is. For he shall be as a tree planted by the waters, and that spreadeth out her roots by the river, and shall not see when heat cometh, but her leaf shall be green; and shall not be careful in the year of drought, neither shall cease from yielding fruit."*

When individuals go through the curriculum of Reformers Unanimous, it helps them resolve their personal and Spiritual conflicts. After this, I counsel them to seek as much prayer support as possible. In addition, I strongly recommend that those who come to us at Reformers Unanimous involve a trusted friend so that together they may bathe the entire process in prayer. We pray in faith. We know that the Lord is *"upon me; because the LORD hath anointed me to preach good tidings unto the meek; he hath sent me to bind up the brokenhearted, to proclaim liberty to the captives, and the opening of the prison to them that are bound;"* (Isaiah 61:1). As we pray, God gives us the strength to not be discouraged but to persevere until we allow the Holy Spirit complete control of our lives. Discouragement is one of Satan's most effective weapons. He wants us to give up on God and disbelieve that Christ is willing and able to make us free. We are often like the man Mark tells about whose son was terribly demonized. He pleaded with Jesus. Mark 9:22 – *"And ofttimes it hath cast him into the fire, and into the waters, to destroy him: but if thou canst do any thing, have compassion on us, and help us."* Jesus said to him, *"If thou canst believe, all things are possible to him that believeth. And straightway the father of the child cried out, and said with tears, Lord, I believe; help thou mine unbelief"* (Mark 9:23-24). Jesus quickly set the boy free and later explained to the disciples the reason for the failure of their earlier attempt to help the boy. Mark 9:29 – *"And he said unto them, This kind can come forth by nothing, but by prayer and fasting."* Prayer and fasting demonstrates our dependence upon God.

Be honest with God. If you are struggling with unbelief, tell God your faith is weak, and ask Him to help your unbelief. Take a proactive approach to pulling together an army of prayer warriors who will call upon the Lord Jesus Christ and claim the fact that the power of sin and Satan in your life has been broken.

Consider these powerful prayer promises:

Matthew 21:21-22 – *"Jesus answered and said unto them, Verily I say unto you, If ye have faith, and doubt not, ye shall not only do this which is done to the fig tree, but also if ye shall say unto this mountain, Be thou removed, and be thou cast into the sea; it shall be done. And all things, whatsoever ye shall ask in prayer, believing, ye shall receive."*

John 15:7 – *"If ye abide in me, and my words abide in you, ye shall ask what ye will, and it shall be done unto you."*

John 14:12-14 – *"Verily, verily, I say unto you, He that believeth on me, the works that I do shall he do also; and greater works than these shall he do; because I go unto my Father. And whatsoever ye shall ask in my name, that will I do, that the Father may be glorified in the Son. If ye shall ask any thing in my name, I will do it."*

We realize that Holy Spirit control is God's will for us. So, don't believe the devil's lie that God will help others and not you. If you are a child of God, *"it is God which worketh in you both to will and to do of his good pleasure"* (Philippians 2:13).

Is it God's will for you to be free from anger's control? Of course it is! Know and choose to believe that you can do all things through Christ who strengthens you. Philippians 4:13 – *"I can do all things through Christ which strengtheneth me."*

Holy Spirit control is a fruit of the Spirit according to Galatians 5:22-23 – *"But the fruit of the Spirit is love, joy, peace, longsuffering, gentleness, goodness, faith, Meekness, temperance: against such there is no law."* To keep a deed of the flesh from manifesting itself, stop and pray and ask the Lord to fill you with His Spirit, and then believe that He has.

STEP FOUR – I openly and honestly place myself on the

Great Physician's examination table so that His Holy Spirit may reveal to me my ungodly anger along with the lies that I have believed that have kept me in my ungodly anger.

At first glance, asking God to reveal our inner condition seems extremely frightening. There is no need to fear the truth, especially when the truth is revealed by our loving, compassionate Heavenly Father. In placing ourselves upon God's examination table, we are, in essence, giving the Holy Spirit the keys to every "room" in the house of our lives. We are granting God permission to go everywhere in our past and present, even if it means discovering the skeletons in our closets. We are admitting that we don't have all the answers to our anger problems, but He does. God can make the perfect diagnosis and prescribe the perfect treatment.

I have found it quite amazing how the Spirit of God often reveals the hidden root cause of my problems; root causes that I had totally forgotten or had not considered important before.

If we do not go to God in a proper frame of mind, we can become very defensive when the Holy Sprit reveals certain things in our lives. If we go to God in the proper frame of mind, that is submission to Him and His Word, the Spirit of God can open our eyes and reveal the fear and disapproval of others that exists in our lives. We are bound and determined to present an image of ourselves that was so likeable and efficient that nobody could ever criticize it. However, all the phobias we have in our lives are rooted in lies. We believe that we needed the approval of others in order to accept ourselves. We came to realize that our anger was a defense mechanism designed to protect this false image whenever it was threatened by others' words. What we need to do is renounce the lies and choose to believe the truth that we are already loved and accepted in Christ. It will take time for this mind to be fully renewed and our behaviors transformed, but we would not even be on the right track were it not for our eagerness to allow the Holy Spirit of God to reveal the wrong behaviors in our lives.

STEP FIVE – I choose to open my heart to Christ's compassionate healing touch. I do that by choosing to forgive others with whom I am angry, including myself and God.

This step may be the most powerful liberating for you. Making the choice to forgive ourselves and others from the heart is almost without exception a major stepping stone toward experiencing freedom from anger's control. Forgiving from the heart is a crucial step. Once you forgive others from your heart, don't be surprised that days, weeks and even months later people come to mind that you need to forgive. The Lord will help you recover one layer at a time. If this happens, it in no way invalidates the work that you have already accomplished. It simply means that the Lord is continuing to reveal areas of bondage layer by layer. He knows how much we can handle at any certain moment. If any other issues involving forgiveness do come up, you know what to do. Simply make the choice to forgive from the heart in accordance with the Word of God. Don't become anxious about issues that remain unrevealed. You are responsible to deal with only what you know. Wait for the Lord. Be patient with His timing. He desires your freedom even more than you do, and He *"worketh in you both to will and to do of his good pleasure"* (Philippians 2:13).

Sometimes, after faithfully following the guidelines for forgiving from the heart, you may still feel anger toward those who have offended you. You may wonder if you were sincere in your forgiveness. If this occurs, ask God to search your heart again. Often, there are things that have not been dealt with at all or visited only superficially. Many times we bypass the emotional core because the feelings seem too painful to face. If this happens, God will guide you through the forgiveness process again. Having another person praying with you will help ensure you are being thorough and honest. It is also possible that your anger may be justified, and God wants you to take action to correct the wrong. Many times, however, even after we have forgiven an offender, a deeper healing work needs to take place. Your emotions are damaged, and you need the

Lord Jesus' healing touch in order for you to be whole.

I have seen the Lord do a dramatic work of healing in my life in response to a heart cry for His touch. He will do the same for you as well when you make the choice to forgive.

STEP SIX – At this time, through the leadership of the Holy Spirit, I fully confess and repent of all my ungodly anger. I renounce the lies that I have accepted as truth that have fueled my anger.

Jesus said that it is the truth that makes us free from our slavery to sin. John 8:32 – *"And ye shall know the truth, and the truth shall make you free."* That being true, it is lies that keep us in bondage to sin, whether it is controlling anger, rage, or any other sin of the flesh. There is always at least one lie that keeps us chained to that sinful behavior. It is imperative that your repentance come from the heart. Psalm 24:3-5 – *"Who shall ascend into the hill of the LORD? or who shall stand in his holy place? He that hath clean hands, and a pure heart; who hath not lifted up his soul unto vanity, nor sworn deceitfully. He shall receive the blessing from the LORD, and righteousness from the God of his salvation."*

Allow me to give you some common lies that result in angry attitudes and behavior:

1. No one loves me, not even God.
2. I can't do anything right.
3. I am a failure.
4. I will never amount to anything.
5. I have no talents, gifts or anything to offer.
6. I don't fit in.
7. I am on my own in this world.
8. I have to take care of myself.
9. God will not defend me.
10. God has forgotten me.
11. I cannot trust anyone.
12. I cannot be free.

13. There is no hope for me.
14. The Christian life does not work for me.
15. I am dirty.
16. I am evil.
17. I must be perfect to be accepted.
18. I must be perfect to accept myself.
19. I must never show weakness or let others beat me.
20. I must prove to others I am competent.
21. I must control others to be safe.
22. I am alone.
23. I must perform at a certain level in order to feel good about myself.

It is essential once you renounce lies, such as I stated above that have controlled you, that you replace those lies with the truth. Rehearsing the truth again and again until it is firmly entrenched in our minds will make us free. We must let the peace of Christ rule in our hearts, and we do that by letting the Word of God richly dwell within us. Colossians 3:15-16 – *"And let the peace of God rule in your hearts, to the which also ye are called in one body; and be ye thankful. Let the word of Christ dwell in you richly in all wisdom; teaching and admonishing one another in psalms and hymns and spiritual songs, singing with grace in your hearts to the Lord."*

The truths of who we are in Christ are well worth realizing and meditating upon so that our minds will be renewed according to Romans 12:2 – *"And be not conformed to this world: but be ye transformed by the renewing of your mind, that ye may prove what is that good, and acceptable, and perfect, will of God."*

STEP SEVEN – I ask my Heavenly Father to forgive me for using my body as an instrument of ungodly anger. Having done that, I now present my body to God as an instrument of righteousness.

One of the biggest things we need to do in our lives is to fully surrender to the Lord Jesus Christ in every aspect of our lives. We need to begin to draw upon the Spirit of God to live our lives. Romans 6:11-13 provides the Biblical basis for such a life-changing decision. *"Likewise reckon ye also yourselves to be dead indeed unto sin, but alive unto God through Jesus Christ our Lord. Let not sin therefore reign in your mortal body, that ye should obey it in the lusts thereof. Neither yield ye your members as instruments of unrighteousness unto sin: but yield yourselves unto God, as those that are alive from the dead, and your members as instruments of righteousness unto God."*

Instead of obeying sin's lustful cries that lead to bondage, we need to surrender to God's way that leads to freedom.

STEP EIGHT – I choose to take every thought captive to the obedience of Christ through the putting on of the whole armor of God.

Satan takes advantage of our bitterness and magnifies it into out-of-control rage and revenge. The devil is a liar, deceiver, and accuser. John 8:44 – *"Ye are of your father the devil, and the lusts of your father ye will do. He was a murderer from the beginning, and abode not in the truth, because there is no truth in him. When he speaketh a lie, he speaketh of his own: for he is a liar, and the father of it."* Revelation 12:9-10 – *"And the great dragon was cast out, that old serpent, called the Devil, and Satan, which deceiveth the whole world: he was cast out into the earth, and his angels were cast out with him. And I heard a loud voice saying in heaven, Now is come salvation, and strength, and the kingdom of our God, and the power of his Christ: for the accuser of our brethren is cast down, which accused them before our God day and night."*

Satan seeks to manipulate our emotions and behaviors by controlling our thinking with distorted ideas about God, ourselves and others. Jesus came to destroy the devil's works. I John 3:8 – *"He that committeth sin is of the devil; for the devil sinneth from the beginning. For this purpose the Son of God was manifested, that he might destroy the works of the devil."* Satan was disarmed and defeated at the cross. Colossians 2:15 – *"And having spoiled principalities and powers, he made a shew of them openly, triumphing over them in it."* Since Jesus Christ now has all authority in Heaven and on earth, when we resist the devil, he has to flee from us. James 4:7 – *"Submit yourselves therefore to God. Resist the devil, and he will flee from you."*

Resistance requires active participation on our part. We have to put on the armor of God, stand firm, and resist. The Bible in Ephesians 6:12 tells us, *"For we wrestle not against flesh and blood, but against principalities, against powers, against the rulers of the darkness of this world, against spiritual wickedness in high places."* We are wrestling against demonic powers. To wrestle implies "a struggle requiring energy, focus, and skill." This battle is neither waged nor won on a fleshly level. II Corinthians 10:3 – *"For though we walk in the flesh, we do not war after the flesh:"*

God has mercifully given us His armor of truth, righteousness, peace, salvation, faith, and the Word of God, so that we can wage a victorious battle in prayer against the enemy's schemes. Ephesians 6:10-20 – *"Finally, my brethren, be strong in the Lord, and in the power of his might. Put on the whole armour of God, that ye may be able to stand against the wiles of the devil. For we wrestle not against flesh and blood, but against principalities, against powers, against the rulers of the darkness of this world, against spiritual wickedness in high places. Wherefore take unto you the whole armour of God, that ye may be able to withstand in the evil day, and having done all, to stand. Stand therefore, having your loins girt about with truth, and having on the breastplate of righteousness; And your feet shod with the preparation of the gospel of peace; Above all, taking the shield of faith, wherewith ye shall be able to quench all the fiery darts of the wicked. And take the helmet of salvation, and the sword of the Spirit, which is the word of God: Praying always with all prayer and supplication in the Spirit, and watching thereunto with all perseverance and supplication for all saints; And for me, that utterance may be given unto me, that I may open my mouth boldly, to make known the mystery of the gospel, For which I am an ambassador in bonds: that therein I may speak boldly, as I ought to speak."* But, we must make the choice to put on and take up these weapons. Satan is an exploiter. You give him an inch, and he will take a mile.

By submitting to God in confession and repentance, you will be taking back any ground that Satan may claim as his own in your life. You are, in essence, closing and locking the doors and windows. By resisting the devil, you are turning on the lights and grabbing your weapons to drive any spiritual intruders off of your property. You can be assured that a Heavenly security guard will be dispatched to set a watch over your house. Once the spiritual strongholds of anger and rage have been broken, it is critical that you learn to take every thought captive in obedience to Christ. A large part of this process is guarding what comes into your heart and mind.

Paul advises us in Philippians 4:8 – *"Finally, brethren, whatsoever things are true, whatsoever things are honest, whatsoever things are just, whatsoever things are pure, whatsoever things are lovely, whatsoever things are of good report; if there be any virtue, and if there be any praise, think on these things."*

After surrendering fully to Jesus, you will be convicted over some of the television shows and books you have formerly tolerated and even enjoyed. Your anger is now being replaced by a growing peace and joy as you immerse yourself in the Word of God.

STEP NINE – I desire to reconcile with and make restitution with those I have wounded in my anger. I do this whenever it is possible and wise to do so.

Choosing the path of humility will go against your fleshly feelings. It is one of the more significant steps to freedom when orchestrated by the Holy Spirit. God gives grace to the humble. Relationships that we have damaged or destroyed through our sinful anger can often be repaired and restored. Ultimately, this is God's work. Our responsibility, however, is to be obedient to the Lord and seek reconciliation and healing. Romans 12:8 says, *"Or he that exhorteth, on exhortation: he that giveth, let him do it with simplicity; he that ruleth, with diligence; he that sheweth mercy, with cheerfulness."*

Reconciliation is not always dependent upon us. Another person can refuse to be reconciled to you even after you have prayed, humbly admitted your wrong doing, and reached out in love. The restoration we desire to happen immediately may take time, or it may never happen. When God prompts you to go do your part, you must go regardless of the outcome. Matthew 5:23-24 provides Biblical guidelines for seeking reconciliation with another person – *"Therefore if thou bring thy gift to the altar, and there rememberest that thy brother hath ought against thee; Leave there thy gift before the altar, and go thy way; first be reconciled to thy brother, and then come and offer thy gift."*

This is serious business with God. If we have hurt another person with our anger or rage, we need to go to that person and make restitution. If distance is a problem, a phone call is the next best thing. We don't recommend writing a letter or using email as such communication can be easily misread, misunderstood, passed on to the wrong people, and even used against you legally. If you think your well-being might be jeopardized by going to the other person alone, take someone with you. Private, angry thoughts you've had toward another person that have not resulted in action must be dealt with privately before the Lord.

Be willing to suffer the consequences of your wrongdoing. This may be part of God's breaking and healing of you. Pray and ask God for the right words, attitude, and timing. Make sure you have already forgiven the other party if he or she offended you.

When confessing your misdeeds, label your action as wrong. Be specific and admit what you did. Make no defenses or excuses. Don't blame the other person or demand an apology. That is between him or her and God. Ask specifically, "Will you forgive me?" Wait for the answer. Trust God for the outcome no matter what it is.

CONCLUSIONARY THOUGHT: The nine steps covered above provide a framework through which the Spirit of God can break down the strongholds of anger and make you free. Freedom will be maintained and growth gained as you continue to cultivate an intimate, dynamic relationship with the Living God through consistent worship, prayer, Bible study, and Bible meditation. You also need to intentionally pursue open, honest fellowship with other believers in Christ who will pray for you and your struggle with anger.

Please, remember this: Our Heavenly Father loves you just as much as He loves the Lord Jesus Christ.

Overcoming anger is a life-long process. There will always be new people and circumstances that will test us and push our buttons. Pressures and stresses will come, but Jesus has already overcome the world, the flesh, and the devil. John 16:32-33 – *"Behold, the hour cometh, yea, is now come, that ye shall be scattered, every man to his own, and shall leave me alone: and yet I am not alone, because the Father is with me. These things I have spoken unto you, that in me ye might have peace. In the world ye shall have tribulation: but be of good cheer; I have overcome the world."*

MORE BOOKS FROM REFORMERS UNANIMOUS

THE UMBRELLA FELLA (Code: CE-123 Price: $12.00)

Within every believer's heart is a desire to be all that God would have us to be. But, how can we be what God wants us to be, when we cannot even do the things God wants us to do? *Umbrella Fella* will help us understand our position in the Kingdom of Heaven's chain of command. Once we understand our position, it will forever change our disposition. It all begins with a two letter preposition, the little word, "IN".

TODAY I LAY (Code: CE-124 Price: $9.00)

Seldom does a day go by that we are not faced with the opportunity to die to self. Most every believer recognizes their personal responsibility to put their own wishes and wants on the altar and to sacrifice himself for the cause of Christ. However, God expects much more than a daily dying to self in order to qualify for the power of His resurrection. For us to experience this supernatural power on our lives, we must be willing to not only die for Christ, but to die with Him, be buried with Him and then be raised to walk with Him as we engage in a regular evaluation of our personal "DBR".

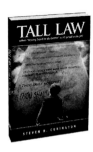

TALL LAW (Code: CE-117 Price: $12.00)

There are two types of Christian life - the abundant life and the redundant life. One is a life of restful service while the other is a life of discouraging works. How do you attain the real deal? You must understand the foundational truths of behavior modification. If you don't then you will have to live your life in your power rather that the power of God - and that's a mighty *Tall Law*.

order online www.reformu.com or call 815.986.0460

WHY IS EVERYBODY CRYING (Code: CE-118 Price: $7.00)

Most every Christian understands that they cannot be possessed. But yet they still find themselves doing things that make them sure the devil made them do it. How does this happen? Very simple…demonic oppression. Learn how Satan uses outside pressure (oppression) to render God's people discouraged and apathetic in their God-given responsibilities in life.

PRODUCE THE JUICE (Code: CE-121 Price: $16.00)

Bro. Curington's newest book, *Produce the Juice*, references the motivational stimulation that a gifted believer experiences when the Holy Spirit exercises His gift(s) that He has placed within the believer. In this book Brother Curington shows how using your gift produces great joy and excitement in the life of a believer. (Comes with a spiritual gifts test CD)

JOURNALS AND CURRICULUM

"IT'S PERSONAL" DAILY JOURNAL – Classic Size (Code: CE-111 Price: $15.00)

The 90-day, *"It's Personal" Daily Journal* is a proven method for developing a dynamic love relationship with Jesus Christ. The journal is our #1 selling product in America! It comes complete with a CD explaining how to use the journal and its five forms of communication with God. (Classic size - 7 x 8 1/2)

"IT'S PERSONAL" DAILY JOURNAL – Full Size (Code: CE-116 Price: $17.00)

A larger version of our 90-day, *"It's Personal" Daily Journal. This version of our* #1 selling product in America is for those who have more to write as they develop a personal love relationship with Christ. It comes complete with a CD explaining how to use the journal and its five forms of communication with God. (Full size - 8 1/2 x 11)

order online www.reformu.com or call 815.986.0460

PERSONAL RECOVERY KIT
(Code: KIT-001 Price: $99.00)

The Personal Recovery Kit is an affordable recovery plan that you can use in the privacy of your own home, without disrupting your daily life. It's an easy to use recovery and training program that will motivate and empower you toward complete recovery. This program has been successful for countless people and we're confident that you will feel healthier and happier and you'll be convinced that your life is changing, for the better!

The Personal Recovery Kit is not a 12-step plan or hypnosis. Addictions are the result of bad decisions, and wrong thinking. In this program, spiritual and medical addiction experts will explain to you how to deal with your bad decisions and wrong thinking. This program will work for any addiction: drugs, alcohol, pornography, tobacco, sexual addiction, eating disorders, cutting, huffing, etc.

The Personal Recovery Kit Package includes:
-Topical Addiction Recovery Book (15 topics to choose from alcohol, cocaine, eating disorders, etc.)
-Spiritual Recovery Journal w/ instructional CD
-Spiritual Recovery Textbook
-10 Spiritual Recovery Principles DVD
-Spiritual Recovery Program Workbook
-Bitterness and Forgiveness Recovery Series MP3 CD
-Spiritual Recovery Mega-Pack MP3 CD (Includes topical teaching on: wrong thinking, depression, forgiveness, RX addiction, sexual addiction, opiates, and dozens of other topics)

order online www.reformu.com or call 815.986.0460